# Introduction

The assassination of President John Fitzgerald Kennedy was staged. President Kennedy did not die in Dallas on November 22, 1963. Someone did, but it was not the president.

Many people and entities were unhappy with President Kennedy's stances on a variety of issues. The unions were unhappy with the direction Kennedy's administration and Attorney General was proceeding with the treatment of union bosses and controlling their behavior. The mob was similarly upset with the treatment it was getting by the President and his brother Bobby. Both organizations had been pumping a significant amount of money into the campaigns of politicians, mainly Democrats, and expected the quid pro quo that they felt they deserved and were paying for.

The President's own party was disappointed with some of his moderate views. A contingent of Democratic insiders was blaming the centralist views on Kennedy's religious ties to the Catholic Church. Others were berating his youth.

Within the executive circle, Vice President Johnson was pushing the President to get more involved in the Vietnam conflict. Kennedy was leaning toward pulling out. He was already labelled an appeaser by the press and public because of how he handled Cuba. Johnson felt that the Soviet aggression needed to be stopped within the Asian continent. Then, when the Bay of Pigs turned out poorly for the United States and Soviet missiles were aimed at the United States mainland with Florida less than one hundred miles away, Johnson was looking for ways to push the Soviets back into Russia.

While Kennedy's storybook, Camelot, rise to the Presidency garnered the love and admiration of the country, unhappiness with Kennedy on multiple fronts was strongly felt by his inner circle.

All presidents since Abraham Lincoln had to contend with the threat of assassination. Attention was refocused to this potential after the assassination of President McKinley. Therefore, every threat that was received was treated as credible. Prior to the trip to Dallas, communications spiked regarding credible threats. There was a significant amount of behind-the-scenes activity related to the threats received by the Secret Service.

When President Kennedy decided to ride in a parade in his honor through the streets of Dallas in an open convertible, and announced it to the public, the Secret Service cringed as the threats began peaking. The head of the President's Secret Service detail pleaded with him to either change his mind or ride in a vehicle that was less exposed. Kennedy said no. After the Bay of Pigs episode and other difficult events, his contact with the American people would help ground him with the public and media.

At the last minute, his presidential decoy replaced him in the convertible in Dallas. The body-double was killed and President Kennedy survived, resulting in the necessity for Kennedy to be hidden from the public for the rest of his life.

The only remaining trace of DNA of the imposter's existence is on a strawberry pink Chanel suit. This suit, as specified in the will of Caroline Kennedy, is being entombed in the National Archives until 2103.

In 2013, in the year of the fiftieth anniversary of the Dallas shooting, several books of memoirs were made public by the Secret Service, written in the hand of President Kennedy. After Kennedy's death, the memoirs were found by Secret Service agents and stored away. The Secret Service did not want them getting out into the public as they would blow the cover of their Presidential Decoy program. Then, in 2012, the Secret Service conducted a thorough review of the entire program. The final report concluded that because of the evolution of biometric, photographic, and forensic technologies, it was no longer possible to create a body double that would pass modern identification techniques. Therefore, they decided to disband the program. The first set of documents they declassified were Kennedy's memoires, which included letters to both the Republican and Democratic National Committees.

Kennedy specified that two copies of his memoires be made and a copy sent to each of the political committees. In his letter to them, he described his participation in the Presidential Decoy program. He also described how he wanted to document his views on politics after his presidency as he felt they could benefit by his 'outsider' views and ultimately make the United States a better place.

Kennedy wrote the letters such that the committee leadership would think they were the only ones that received the letters. He did this to continue the competition, while leveling the playing field. He determined that the party that could figure out how to best use his insights may prevail for a while, but ultimately the pendulum would swing the other way.

The memoirs explain Kennedy's perspective of events leading up to November 22, 1963 ... and events of historical significance and political milestones for the following three decades.

# Chapter 1 – Why Was the Assassination Staged?

Threats to a President's life are common. The guard detail whose job it is to protect the President, the Secret Service, receive threats all the time and handle all threats as they are identified. Many are innocuous, but all are treated as if they are real threats.

In the summer of 1963, the threats on President Kennedy began to become more specific and more prolific. The pieces that the Secret Service put together that there was a threat that was credible. The Secret Service determined that potential perpetrators were looking for an opportunity to capitalize on President Kennedy's passion to mingle and seen by the public. The President liked to be out in the open and relatively unprotected.

The President's relative youth, vigor and reputation were contributors to his strong connection to the people. The connection was measured in exit polling after his presidential win just three years earlier. Kennedy's popularity continued to increase some through the first three years of his presidency, even through some difficult times in dealing with a variety of foreign and domestic issues. Of course, after the Dallas shooting, Kennedy's popularity skyrocketed aided by the painting of "Camelot", carefully brushed on his legacy.

At the beginning of November, the 'chatter' still continued to increase and began to focus on Kennedy's upcoming trip to Dallas, the third week in November. The Secret Service met with President Kennedy on several occasions leading up to the Dallas trip, trying to encourage him to reconsider going. Not only were they concerned with the trip in general, but also one of the items on the agenda was to be a parade through the streets of Dallas. If a parade with many people who could not possible be screened was not bad enough, the President was targeted to ride in a limousine. Moreover, ride in not just any limousine, an open-air limousine.

The Secret Service were brainstorming many ways to try to protect the President as best as they could, planning for all possible potential issues. They knew that the simple fact was – the President would be fully exposed and there was little they could do to protect him.

Finally, the Secret Service personnel were convinced that they would be unsuccessful in getting the trip to Dallas cancelled no matter how hard they tried to convince the President and his advisors. With the mountain of threats they were monitoring, they believed there was a strong possibility that there would be an attempt on the life of the President.

Therefore, four days before the scheduled parade in downtown Dallas, three of the top Secret Service agents met with President Kennedy. They explained to him the dangers of the trip and the intelligence that they had. The President's reaction was, of course, that the trip would not be cancelled. He wanted to show the people that he was still connected to them.  The trip and parade must go on.

The agents understood the President's position, but it was their sworn duty to keep him safe.  Given the environment as they knew it, after about an hour of somewhat heated discussion on both sides, they told the President that they were forced to initiate operation Jack-In-the-Box.

# Chapter 2 –
# Kennedy's Rise to
# Political Power

Before understanding the details underlying Operation Jack-In-the-Box, it is important to spend a few minutes reminding one of how John Kennedy climbed his way up the political ladder to be sitting in the White House in the first place. History was certainly against a young Irish Catholic man rising to the summit of politics to the Oval Office as President of the United States.

Quickly starting from the VERY beginning...

John Fitzgerald Kennedy was born on May 29, 1917. His quick rise to political prominence was fueled, in part, by his father Joe Kennedy's desire to have his children involved in public service. Some sarcastically say Joe was only interested in having political connections to keep the police from catching up to him.

Kennedy's older brother Joe Jr. was initially tagged by the elder Joe as the family's political public official. Unfortunately, Joe

Jr. was killed in August of 1944, less than a year prior to the surrender of Japan. The patriarch of the family then turned to the next eldest son, Jack, to take Joe Jr.'s place in the political fray.

Certainly, one of the factors that made John Kennedy popular was his heroic efforts during WWII and his experience with the United States Navy. He was highly decorated with a Purple Heart and three bronze stars. Kennedy also earned WWII associated medals – the American Defense Service Medal, the American and Asiatic-Pacific Campaign medals and the WWI Victory Medal.

Not even thirty years old, in 1946, Kennedy ran for a vacated seat in the US House to represent his home state of Massachusetts – and won by a large margin. Kennedy served for three terms until 1952, continually increasing his knowledge about the how to get things done in Congress. At that time, Harry Truman was the president, filling the remaining fourth term of Franklin Roosevelt and then winning his own election in 1948.

Following his three-term stint in the House, Kennedy ran for a Massachusetts seat in the US Senate. His political might became stronger as he defeated Henry Cabot Lodge. In 1956, Kennedy was running two races, a reelection to his Senate position and he was tapped to run as a Vice Presidential candidate on the ticket with Adlai Stevenson. Unfortunately for the Stevenson/Kennedy ticket, after twenty-four years of a Democratic monopoly in the White House, they fell short to the war hero, Dwight Eisenhower and his running mate Richard Nixon.

Kennedy's experience during the 1956 Presidential campaign would prove to help prepare him for his run in 1960. Kennedy continued his activities in the Senate, still plagued by his lower back pain that included spinal operations to attempt to curb the pain. One of the bills that Kennedy was prominent on was the 1957 Civil Rights Act. There was a measure of infighting in the Democratic Party between Kennedy and the Senate majority leader, Lyndon Johnson. A compromise was struck, but the interesting relationship between Senator Kennedy and Senator Johnson was obviously not over.

Through 1960, Kennedy campaigned for President. The battle to decide who would challenge the ultimate Republican candidate was very energetic. The major competitors were four Senators – Hubert Humphrey from Minnesota, Lyndon Johnson from Texas, Wayne Morse from Oregon and Kennedy from Massachusetts – along with some other also-rans.

Kennedy had a very strong showing in the primaries and all but eliminated Humphrey and Morse along the way. Therefore, going into the Democratic Convention, his main competitor was Senator Johnson. Kennedy's stage presence and political prowess won the hearts and minds of the delegates. One of the examples of his ability to strike a chord in each of these areas was when he gave his famous New Frontier speech. A highlight of this speech was "… However, the New Frontier of which I speak is not a set of promises – it is a set of challenges. It sums up not what I intend to offer the American people, but what I intend to ask of them."

The concept of encouraging the American people to be self-sufficient, to be challenged to excel rather than relying on someone else, or Government, was a popular and common theme for Kennedy. He was capitalizing on the strong can-do attitude that was pervasive amongst Americans through the war and attempting to continue that mindset to the growth of the country.

# Chapter 3 – Operation Jack-In-the-Box

Presidential Decoy was a Secret Service plan that was modified to be unique for every President since William McKinley.

The plan was not conceived as a charge for the Secret Service as they were formed. In fact, as an interesting side note, the "Secret Service Division" was created by President Lincoln on the day of HIS assassination – April 14, 1865. The Secret Service Division's initial charge was to investigate and reduce counterfeiting. Then after the assassination of President McKinley in 1901, Congress extended the scope of the Secret Service to include guarding the President, a scope that had secretly already been taken on.

Presidential Decoy was initially conceived when it was realized that even through best intentions; there would be situations where the President could not be fully protected. So, beginning with Grover Cleveland in 1886, Mckinley's predecessor, a "Presidential Decoy" was discovered to fill in for the President when security warranted its use.

The existence of the decoy was a secret that was so well protected that even the wives of the President did not know of them. This was partially because the decoy was very rarely used. In the late 1980's and early 1900's, even though the decoy looked like the President, he was not an exact match. In the rare instances where the decoy was used, it was in a situation where the President did not need to talk and was going to be situated quite a ways from photographers and people who may recognize any differences. It was very difficult to find someone who not only looked like the President, but also could talk like him.

Through the 1900's technology got increasingly better. The make-up that was used to mimic the looks of the President led to plastic surgery. Through voice training and larynx manipulations, the Presidential imposter was able to sound more like the President. Since it was this person's job to stand in for the President of the United States, he was trained every day to pick up every mannerism of the commander in chief – from how he walks, to how he ties his shoes, to how he dances with his wife. The President's wife even has a stand in. Although, the wife's stand in is not for the purpose of being a body double, but to be someone for the President's double to practice with. The ultimate goal of the decoy was that no one would be able to detect that the stand in was not the President – not even the First Lady.

By 1960, the technology that was used was very advanced. A double was selected even before John Kennedy won the election. In fact, a double was also selected for Richard Nixon, who Kennedy defeated, just in case he was needed. The selected decoy already bore a striking resemblance to the dashing Massachusetts senator.

Little manipulation needed to be done. Lose a few pounds, change your walk a little, the physical characteristics were easy. The difficulty was the voice. It took over six months of constant focus before the double's voice could pass as Kennedy voice. That

11

strong Massachusetts dialect and inflection was difficult to manage for a man from the Midwest.

Then, the other difficultly was to train him to demand the attention of every room he walked into. The confidence and power that Kennedy oozed when he was interacting with others proved very difficult to emulate by someone to whom it did not come naturally. Finally, the decoy was ready but the practice did not stop. The double needed to be constantly briefed on what was going on day by day. If he was going to impersonate the President, he had to know what the President knew and be prepared to respond to any situation that may arise as the President would. Some 'miscues' could be tolerated because they could be downplayed with a claim of a headache or a flip "no big deal" response. Too many miscues would call into doubt the double's authenticity.

As the summer of 1963 began and the threats against the President were increasing, the importance also increased of making certain the decoy (of course, they called him Jack and Mr. President so he could get used to it) was ready. Up until now, there was no need for the Decoy Jack to be conscripted into service, but he had to be always at the ready. The beginnings of Operation "Jack-In-the-Box" were under way.

This readiness is like the back-up quarterback always at the ready in case the quarterback gets hurt. It also resembles the man at the switch at the Nike missile silo. Ready to engage the missile at a moment's notice, but hoping you never have to exercise your training.

## November 18, 1963

*This evening, Frank wanted to see me. I thought it was a bit odd, because he is generally on his way home to have dinner with his family. Nevertheless, this day was different. Frank met me in the side office from the Oval office. No one else was around. He reiterated many of the concerns that he and his compatriots have had for my safety, including the many threats on my life. I stopped him not too far into his seemingly prepared remarks and asked him to cut to the chase. My back was twinging from all the sitting I did today. I did not have much opportunity to even walk around and stretch my legs.*

*He then began to explain a plan that has been in effect since William McKinley to keep President's safe. He explained that there is someone that looks and talks just like me. He said that this person is trained to stand in for me in case the Secret Service feels they would not be able to protect me adequately. He said that they wanted to send him to Dallas in my place. He said that if something happened and the other Jack was seriously wounded, or nothing happened, that the switch back could quickly happen and I could go back to normal operations.*

*About a million questions were flying through my head. Who is this guy? Why did I not know he existed? Where is he? Does he really look like me? How could he fool the American people? How could he fool Jackie?*

*Several of these questions began spewing from my mouth. Finally, Frank interrupted. He said, "Mr. President, tomorrow we will take you to meet Jack."*

## November 19, 1963

*Today I met Jack, my decoy. I had my calendar blocked off and we flew to Camp David for the meeting – Jack was already there. It was a surreal experience. As we first met, he began by repeating everything I said. "Nice to meet you." "Nice to meet you." "Thank you for your service." "Thank you for your service." "How did you learn to talk like me?" "How did you learn to talk like me?"*

*After several more pleasantries, Frank explained that "Jack" had been training about two years to be able to stand in for me if the moment arose. He asked if I would participate in part of the day's training, and I agreed. They built the training up to asking questions about what I knew about Dallas, the people, the sites, any of Lyndon's acquaintances I knew.*

*It was a very thorough interaction. I am not certain if the session was for "Jack" or me, but I left Camp David that morning feeling that if I needed a stand-in, this was a man that could pull it off.*

Both Tuesday and Wednesday night, Kennedy tossed and turned in bed. The Camp David meeting was weighing heavily on him. He knew that if the double replaced him and was shot, the guilt of putting someone in harm's way like that, knowing that there may be negative consequences, was difficult for an ex-military man to absorb. It was the same pause that the President had every time he sent a young soldier to war, but now it was much more personal.

## November 20, 1963

*I could not sleep. Jackie asked several times what was on my mind. I am not certain exactly how I responded, but I am certain it was not what was really on my mind. How can artificially preserving my life be for the good of the country? Just like my days cruising the Pacific, you take a job knowing the risks going in. When one of the risks presents itself, you accept it – you make the best of it. You do not hide.*

The thought of the decoy being killed, was almost more than he could bear. His conclusion when he woke up on the 21st was that he would not let the other Jack take his place. It was he that the public was going to come out to see.

On Thursday morning, November 21, the head of the President's secret service detail approached the President. He told Kennedy that they needed to implement operation "Jack-In-The-Box". At first, the President refused, recalling the bantering back and forth that went on in his head the past two nights. After fifteen

14

minutes of discussion that seemed like hours, Kennedy relinquished to the pressure of the Secret Service.

The plan was that the President would skip the trip to Dallas and be bunkered down in a secret hiding place that very few people in the world even knew existed. It was in a suburb of Washington, a short drive away.

The plan was that on Friday morning, the switch would happen just before boarding the helicopter to be transported to Air Force One waiting at Edwards Air Force base.

## November 21, 1963

*Against my initial judgment, I am going to follow the suggestion of Frank. I understand that he is doing his job – to protect the President of the United States.*

*At a certain point, the President is more than just a man. The president is a symbol of the greatest country that the world has ever seen - The benevolent giant that serves as a beacon of hope in the fog of reality.*

*I only wish that I could face the situation like a man – instead of facing it like a figurehead.*

On Friday morning, President Kennedy got up and went through his routine as normal as he could. Jackie seemed to sense that he was a bit distant in his thoughts. Her husband attributed it to a bit of nerves in preparation for his speech in Dallas. He said he had not prepped for it as much as he had hoped, but told her he would work on it on the plane on the way to Dallas. As he normally does, Kennedy took care of some presidential business in the office while Jackie was finishing getting dressed. The switch was made and the President was whisked away to the secret hiding place in a service vehicle that had just made a food delivery to the White House while the decoy took over his life for a day. The plan was that after the speech and returning to the White House, that they would switch back and no one would be the wiser.

President Kennedy was joking with the secret service detail that accompanied him to the secret bunker. He said that he had not done a final practice of the speech as he normally does because he knew he did not have to deliver it today. He compared it to not studying for a test when you are certain it is going to snow and school will be called off.

As the President was comfortably resting in the bunker, the President's double was on the plane. He was a bit quieter than the President normally is. He explained that he was doing some last minute preparation for his speech. Kennedy's need to practice that he told Jackie earlier in the morning was a piece of last minute information that was passed along to the double team.

Air Force One landed in Dallas about noon on November 22nd. "Jack" had pulled off the charade so far. He had apparently fooled the reporters on the plan, his inner circle, and even Jackie, although she did not interact with him too much. She was lost in a book she was reading and tried to leave him alone to do his "President" work. The next challenge was to fool the American people.

"Jack" stopped at a microphone after deplaning from Air Force One. He looked exactly like the President – could he sound like the President? To break the tight grip of nerves that were grasping his throat, "Jack" cracked a joke about Jackie's tardiness of coming down the stairs of the plane, attributing it to her need to be beautiful. The resulting laughter worked to loosen up his throat.

About ninety minutes later, the decoy was dead and Jackie Kennedy, her children John and Caroline, the Kennedy family a nation and world - began to mourn.

# Chapter 4 – After the Assassination

After the shooting and the body was loaded into Air Force One, Vice President Johnson was sworn into the Presidency. It was an orderly transition and the United States had its 36th President. In parallel with the swearing in ceremony and as Air Force One was streaking back to Washington D.C., there was another discussion happening, this one in in Washington – the Secret Service notified Kennedy that the Presidential decoy had been shot – and killed. Kennedy was in shock. Just as a million questions were running through his head when the idea of Jack-In-the-Box was described to him, now his thinking shifted to "what now?"

The Secret Service took immediate control of the decoy's body. They did not want any physical evidence to linger or leak out that an imposter was the one that took the bullet. DNA testing had not yet been utilized for forensic autopsies, but there may be ways – dental or others – for keen medical examiners to question.

The Secret Service arranged for the body to be taken directly to Bethesda Naval Hospital for the autopsy. Commanders Boswell and Humes (MC, USN) performed the autopsy on the decoy's body. During the autopsy, all physical evidence was secured and protected.

## November 22, 1963

*I – at least in the eyes of the world – was assassinated. I am now told that no one can ever know that I am still alive, for fear that the power of the United States would be irreversibly disrupted – and to protect the lives of future Presidents. The burden I now face is that I will never be able to communicate with my wife, my children, my family, or my friends.*

*The bullet that was meant for me should have succeeded. If God's will was for me to leave this Earth and the good that I attempted to leave behind, then why was God's will not done? What will my life be like? Am I now destined to be imprisoned in a body that essentially does not exist?*

*I asked Frank about Jackie and the kids. He said that he did not know very much, but knew that she was safe and unharmed by the shooting. The whole episode is likely not perceived yet by the children.*

*I am very aware of the country's succession process. I did not ask Frank, but I am certain Lyndon was sworn in as soon as humanly possible.*

*I think he has likely kicked himself for the last three years for losing to me in the primary. I hope that my agenda was not too different from what he will institute. Godspeed, Lyndon – Mr. President [handwriting was shaky].*

*Frank said that tomorrow we would be travelling to my permanent residence. When I pressed him as to where my final resting place would be, he said – California. Frank explained that I needed to stay out of the public eye - in fact, out of sight. He said that since everyone in the world had thought I was dead, if I were to show up somewhere and be recognized it could cause havoc. It would not only be disruptive to Jackie and the children, but to the country and even the world. Protecting Presidents in the future may get to be that much more difficult and there would be a Constitutional crisis regarding who should be President.*

The Secret Service Presidential Decoy operation was thorough and complete. A bunker home was created in the side of a hill overlooking the Pacific Ocean in southern California. The portion of the home that was visible was relatively small and meant not to attract attention. A husband and wife family was living in the front portion of the bunker, serving as the front for the operation and caretaker if, heaven forbid, the bunker needed to be used. The larger area extended into the hill, providing protection, security and, unfortunately, solace.

Kennedy would not be the first "special guest" of the bunker. William McKinley spent almost twelve years in the bunker until he died in 1913 at the age of 70 – over a decade later than his assassination in September of 1901.

In the 50's, the bunker was renovated. World War II had reminded the Secret Service executives in charge of the decoy program of the challenges that the tensions of the day presented. Several new rooms were added, the furnishings were updated, ventilation was enhanced and sub-basement was added. The sub-basement was to be used by Secret Service as the West Coast center for operations. Security was also updated as California was growing faster than the Secret Service had anticipated and there were fears of domestic and foreign assault.

## November 23, 1963

*Today, at four o'clock in the morning, we began our journey to California. Frank and two other heavily armed men escorted me on board a Ford motor home. It has no extras, but is*

19

*comfortable. It smells like new, they must have just purchased it. I read the sales brochures and it was a Ford Condor- kitchen, bathroom, shower, bed, table, chairs. At this point, what more do I need?*

## November 24, 1963

*We arrived at my new home. I was impressed by the professionalism of my travel companions. They likely did not fully realize all of what I was going through, but I know this is not easy for them as well. They were asked to transport the President (well, former President) across country without anyone, even their families knowing.*

*During the trip across the country, I had a lot of time to think about my current situation. I feel as though I cheated death. I should have been the one that died in Dallas on Friday. Why was I spared? Is there a master plan for me that I have yet to consider? The Almighty must have a master plan.*

*One option, of course, is to be a hermit and continue to breathe until I do not breathe anymore. While being a hermit may sound like a just penance for cheating death, it is not me. In fact, one way to look at it is that I did not cheat death; the duty of the Secret Service was for the President to avoid it. Had the body double been badly wounded, or if the situation was less public and the Secret Service been able to take control before being declared dead, I would have been able to 'recover' and continue to lead the nation. However, the situation got out of control and I am 'banished' to California.*

*About halfway through the trip, somewhere past the Mississippi river and before the Rocky Mountains, I decided that my calling is still politics. I reached the height of the political circus in the United States. The State of the State is very challenging, and I see how it will need constant care and feeding to maintain the basic principles established by the founding fathers, while morphing to the challenges of modern day life.*

*The common needs of life in the late 1700's were to put a roof over the heads of the children and food in their mouths and opportunities for education. While those are still common problems, society has evolved such that poverty is the exception, not the rule. In addition, for the exception, we have ways to get people back on their feet when situations have interfered with their pursuit of life, liberty and happiness.*

*Today, the common problem does not compare to the past – but the ideals still do. We have moved from sustainment of life, to the betterment of life. We explored the wilderness on horseback, now the possibility of safely landing a man on the moon. There may not be a limit to the creativity of men and women, but I have seen that there could be forces that stand in our way, making us retreat from life, liberty and happiness and allow power to corrupt.*

*I pray that it was not my misuse of power that led a man to aim a gun at me and shoot. If so, I apologize. My primary goal was to leave the office in better shape than when I was given the keys by the American people. I hope that is how I will be remembered.*

*Fortunately, I have been promised that I would not be cut off from news reports, nor paper and pen. Therefore, my pledge to myself and anyone who is interested is to pay attention to what is happening in the world, put a filter on the information that is void of political pressures and document my opinion of what can be done to ensure a balance between our past and our future. This is how I will attempt to give the remaining days of my life some meaning.*

*Not seeing my family is probably the hardest part of this entire endeavor. I am very hopeful that my new focus in life will not only fill a small amount of the void that I have being separated from my loved ones, but perhaps in some way can be used for good.*

## November 25, 1963

*While I am certain I did not receive the full breadth of information about the events of today, I had enough. I am not certain that I ever want to know all the details. Just thinking about what Jackie had to go through is more than I could bear. I should have listened to everyone that said the drive through Dallas was a bad idea. Then, today would be much different.*

*Today, however, is my funeral. I pray that Jackie will be successful in moving on with her life and take good care of John and Caroline, which I know she will. I am sorry, my darlings, that I will not be there to help you, but you are in the best hands you possibly could be. Your mother has a heart big enough for two parents.*

## November 28, 1963

*Thanksgiving was very different this year. We had some turkey and trimmings and watched some football. I do not know if I will ever get used the games being on so early on the west coast. I suppose that is why California is a great place to retire, sporting events are over sooner and the retirees can get to bed sooner.*

*While I have much to be thankful for – the focus of my prayers went with my family and my country.*

## November 30, 1963

*My bunker is very comfortable. I am not forced to hide in a cave as I had initially thought. I do get to see the sun (albeit out of sight of anyone except for those who also reside here). There is a fully stocked library – many history books, of which I plan to take full advantage. I also have an opportunity to read several different newspapers. I have also been assured that we would soon be getting a television. The caretakers of the bunker were never*

*television fans and had no need for one. I am told that we should
be able to a good signal from the television broadcast towers.*

    *Until recent events dictated, there apparently was no need
for too many 'extras'. The furnishings are quite nice. It is not the
White House of the West Coast, but it is very comfortable. I was
told that it was remodeled in the last ten years or so, to keep it
updated. My bedroom is downstairs, so there are not any
windows. However, there is some sort of pipe that goes up
through the hill and to the outside. I am not certain as to how it
works, but it provides some reflected sunlight into my bedroom.
There is also a sunlight pipe that lights up the back rooms. It is
very ingenious, because it gives the impression that you are not
tucked back into a hill.*

    *There is even a room where I can exercise, keep my blood
flowing and back from freezing up on me. Unfortunately, I do not
think my caretakers will be too willing to join me in a game of
football on the beach.*

In December, Congress sent to President Johnson a piece of
legislation titled the Clean Air Act. With the onset of the industrial
revolution in 40-50 years prior to 1963, industries grew with limited
regulations as to the pollutants that were being spewed out of
smokestacks. Not only were they an eyesore, but also there was
increasing empirical evidence that these pollutants were dangerous
to people. In 1955, a Clean Air Act was passed that funded research
aimed at the negative impacts of pollution on public health. The
1963 version of the legislation was specifically designed to control
air pollution throughout the United States by requiring the
Environmental Protection Agency to develop and implement
regulations to control airborne contaminants across the country.

## December 17, 1963

    *I read that Lyndon signed the Clean Air Act today. I am
pleased that this legislation was expanded from the research that*

*was started in the mid-1950s. I read some of the reports from that research and it is clear that if left unchecked, we would be choked out by our own prosperity. Just as now technology is used to enhance human life by building new time-saving and efficient devices, technology should also be developed that protected our air, water and resources. There is a fine line that will likely be crossed going in both directions. This should be a satisfactory occurrence such that the ultimate steady state is not skewed one way or the other.*

*Government regulations should not stifle growth, but also should not let growth maintain dominance over the environment.*

*I recall a speech that I made where I touched on this important research. "For, in the final analysis, our most common link is that we all inhabit this small planet. We all breathe the same air. We all cherish our children's future. And we are all mortal."*

# Chapter 5 – 1964

Disenfranchising voters is not a new idea. It may have been around since the very first time an election was held. Even though the North won the civil war and slaves were freed, there was still a measure of contempt against blacks in the South through the exercise of deep-rooted discrimination. The discrimination was seen in many aspects of life in the South - from rest rooms to voting.

Even though the Fifteenth Amendment to the Constitution was specific in its explanation that race and skin color may not limit a person's right to vote, there were many powerful politicians that wanted to see that blacks were discouraged from voting. States imposed literacy tests and prejudiced citizens threatened violence. Another common method used to discourage the black vote was the institution of a poll tax. The poll tax was simple – if you pay the tax, you can vote. The tax was established to be well out of reach for the typical black voter.

President Kennedy pushed very hard for the Twenty-fourth Amendment to the Constitution, which dealt specifically with the poll tax issue, and any other similar tool used to limit voting to a particular section of citizens. The language was straightforward. "The right of citizens of the United States to vote in any primary or other election for President or Vice President, for electors for President or Vice President, or for Senator or Representative in Congress, shall not be denied or abridged by the United States or any State by reason of failure to pay any poll tax or other tax."

Kennedy calculated that the best way to avoid the notion of abolishing poll taxes without barriers by Congress or the courts was to let the American people vote for an Amendment to the Constitution. Finally, on August 27, 1962 the Amendment passed Congress. As of June 27, 1963, thirty-six States had ratified the amendment. There were only two more needed for ratification.

On January 16, 1964, Maine became the thirty-seventh State to ratify. One week later, on January 23, 1964, South Dakota became the final ratification needed to make the Twenty-fourth Amendment to the Constitution the law of the land.

Mississippi was the only State that rejected the amendment. Four States ratified the amendment many years later. Virginia ratified in 1977, North Carolina in 1989, Alabama in 2002 and Texas in 2009.

Eight States have not ratified the amendment – Arizona, Arkansas, Georgia, Louisiana, Mississippi, Oklahoma, South Carolina, and Wyoming.

## January 24, 1964

*The UPI article today was a very welcome piece of news. "The South Dakota Legislature, beating out Georgia legislators in a race to make history, wrote the anti-poll tax amendment into the United States Constitution today."*

*Finally, the poll tax amendment was ratified. I was hoping that I would live to see the day that discrimination of black voters regarding their rights and opportunity to vote would be diminished – even though Lyndon took the bow.*

*Civil rights is a great challenge for the United States. As there are more generations that separate the current thinking from the thinking in the day of Lincoln, the hope for all races to be treated equally should be more pronounced. Unfortunately, there are too many on both sides of the aisle with legislative pens that are not far enough along in their civil rights thinking.*

*There should not always need to be an Amendment to the Constitution enacted to overcome the discriminations that still exist in the populace. Perhaps as more people see the need for equality and elect politicians of like mind, equality can be exercised by actions and not demanded by law.*

Congress approved the minting of the Kennedy half-dollar a mere month after the shooting, replacing Benjamin Franklin on the front of the current coin. President Johnson called on Congress to pass quickly the resolution that would initiate the needed production to change the minting. Fortunately, for the administrators who managed mint operations, there was already a relief of Kennedy on a Presidential medal that could save time in retaining an artist to create a new relief from scratch. This Presidential medal relief was modified and became the final Kennedy relief for the new fifty-cent coin. By the time Congress passed the bill on December 30, 1963, the first dies were ready four days later on January 3, 1964.

As some may have expected, initial demand for the Kennedy coin far exceeded supply. With all three mints stamping coins, the initial planned release was 91 million. By the end of the minting, the quotas were raised to over 400 million coins.

Another consideration that was not fully calculated was that the 1964 minting called for ninety percent of the coin to be silver. The high percentage of silver and volume of coins minted began to severely deplete the silver stockpiles in the mints. Responding to the silver depletion and the fact that the vast majority of coins were hoarded by collectors rather than allowing them to be circulated, the next year in 1965, the silver content was cut by more than half to 40%.

On December 30, 1970, President Nixon signed a bill that finally eliminated all silver from the coin. It is no wonder that the coins were hoarded. Ninety percent silver at $20 an ounce results in $7.23 value of silver in a single fifty-cent coin. The overall mineral value is a little higher when the value of the 10% copper is included. For what cost you fifty cents in 1964, appreciated by over fourteen times in fifty years.

## January 30, 1964

*Frank really surprised me tonight. We were discussing what we should have for dinner and neither could agree. I wanted a small piece of prime rib, baked potato and a salad and he wanted salmon. After going back and forth a few times, just as we were both relinquishing the decision to each other, he suggested we flip a coin to decide, which I agreed.*

*Frank asked whether I wanted heads or tails and I responded tails. He got an odd grin on his face and removed a coin from his pocket, laid it on his right palm and flipped in up in the air. The light caught the coin as it was tumbling up toward the ceiling and I noticed how shiny it was and thought that it must be new.*

*My mind briefly bounced backwards in time as I thought back to when John and I opened the tin house bank.*

*The coin landed on the ground, flipped a couple of times and Frank quickly announced – "Heads, I win".*

*As I glanced down to verify that salmon was in my near future, I noticed that the coin looked different from any I had seen. I reached down and picked it up. It was my face.*

*My emotions ran the gamut. I was proud that there were people that thought enough of me to enshrine my profile on a coin. However, I was also sad that I was standing in the living room of my bunker in Southern California and the reality was in my hand that the world has resigned me to the stack of dead Presidents.*

President Johnson took some pages from the Kennedy social reform playbook (the New Frontier introduced in JFK's nomination acceptance speech). Johnson's Great Society reforms continued the Kennedy focus on civil rights and racial inequities and poverty.

## May 23, 1964

*Lyndon is pushing his "Great Society" theme. I see he was at Ohio University and then University of Michigan. I am hoping that the New Frontier becomes commonplace – that all people have equal opportunity to meet their goals. This can only come about if the barriers to equality are removed and all Americans respect the tearing down of those boundaries.*

*Several years ago, after I determined that the politicians should lead by example and not always by government fiat in the form a new law. I established the President's Committee on Equal Employment Opportunity. My goal was to eliminate discrimination based on color, religion, or country from which you immigrated. The term "affirmative action" was meant to enforce the active, positive steps that employers must follow to void their hiring of discriminatory practices if they want to continue to do work for the Federal government.*

*A broad policy of equal opportunity should be more than a typical political policy or an election plank. It needs to be embraced as the founders of the country intended. The American experiment relies on the ability of all people to strive to be better, to feel as though they are contributors to society. To do so, the differences from one person to the next should not be based on skin color, gender, or religious preferences. These discriminators must be removed from the thoughts and actions of all people.*

*Equal opportunity is more than a right. In fact, the term "civil rights" may be somewhat dangerous. The farmer does not have the "right" to have a bumper crop every year. Nevertheless, society can assist by helping to clear away the brush from the land, aid in irrigation and see that there is a market for the fruit of the farmer's hard work.*

*The farmer should have the opportunity to succeed, but ultimately it is up to him or her to buy and plant the seeds, enhance the soil, take advantage of the rain, tend to the plants as they grow, and harvest them at the best time to sell.*

The Civil Rights Act of 1964 was a milestone for civil rights. The Act legislated the end of discrimination against differences in race, ethnicities, religion, nationalities, and gender. President Johnson signed the bill into law on July 2, 1964 – less than eight months after taking office.

The Congressional vote was very much divided by remnants of the Civil War. Southerners in the House - 7 of 94 Democratic Representatives voted for the bill and zero of 10 Republicans. Southerners in the Senate – 1 of 21 Democratic Senators voted for the bill and zero of one Republicans. Robert Byrd was the only Northern Democratic Senator to vote against the legislation.

## July 3, 1964

*Bobby must be proud. The Civil Rights Act is now law.*

*Strom [Thurmond] was never really on board as he once called the bill the worst civil right legislation ever put before Congress. Byrd filibustered against it for over 14 hours. I am certain that at some point, Democrats will realize the benefits of treating all of our society equally and with respect, regardless of all differences.*

*It is unfortunate that change must come through legislation. The legislation change is merely a path toward behavior change that may take generations to achieve. When children are taught a behavior based on how their parents act, it does not matter what the parents say, their actions will be what is propagated.*

*Today the racial pendulum is swung much too far toward the direction of exclusion. It may take a few swings back and forth before equilibrium is reached and behaviors are naturally predisposed to make opportunities available to all. It is then up to those that were excluded to take advantage of those opportunities and continue to set the bar high for success.*

President Johnson used the Gulf of Tonkin incident as impetus to ask Congress for a formal declaration of war. There are accounts of a trigger-happy commander of the USS Maddox against what he thought were aggressive North Vietnamese torpedo boats as the rationale for the ultimate war declaration. The naval skirmish happened on August 2nd. President Johnson addressed the nation about the communist aggression via a radio broadcast on August 4th even though later he privately admitted that for all he knew, the navy could have been shooting at whales.

It was almost unanimous. The Senate voted eighty-eight to two and the House vote was 416 to zero to formally declare war on the Viet Cong and North Vietnam.

Ironically, the two rival Senators, Kennedy and Nixon are both part of the history of the Vietnam War. The conflict is historically recognized and beginning under Kennedy's watch (even though the United States had involvement in the conflict as early as the early 1950s) and ended in 1973 under Nixon's watch, with the war officially ending in 1975.

## August 10, 1964

*I pray that the declaration of war in Vietnam will not be the single largest legacy that will befall Lyndon's presidency. Even though he was able to garner the vote of almost the entire Congress, it is a war where the interest of the United States will be questioned.*

*The issues I had with Cuba were a bit different. North Vietnam is not less than a hundred miles from the United States mainland like Cuba is. The proliferation of communism could be a mission better battled by example than force. The more we are able to demonstrate and communicate the benefits of democracy over communism, the better chance change will be sustainable. Rather than the focus being on proliferation of a communist doctrine as the key impetus of involvement, perhaps the banner under which we act should be on helping to ensure that all nations have their own opportunities to choose and do not get stuck in a choice they regret.*

*Lyndon's focus on Vietnam cannot be good for the country. Putting our troops in harm's way the way we are solely in the name of national interest is not how this Country was founded. We cannot be the police of the world. This forces us to take sides. In addition, when we take sides, how are we certain that we are on the right side? If we let the Country fall into the role of police for the world, we run the risk of alienating at least half the world, and maybe more. Obviously, we do not want a situation such as that that pulled us into World War II to ever happen again. Avoiding World War III should be at the paramount of the world's collective thinking.*

*However, we can be a beacon of hope from our actions within our borders. This does not mean isolationism, leading from the medic unit, or closing our borders to immigrants, but rather we should lead from the front, from our actions and our results.*

*We should not force our way of thinking on the world. As we teach our children, they do not listen to our words, but watch our behavior. They do as we do, not as we say. Let the world see for them that the bases for this country are sound and weather the test of time. We have demonstrated and can continue to demonstrate that the American experiment can succeed.*

President Johnson declared a war on poverty in January of 1964. This declaration was based on growing numbers of

Americans in impoverished circumstances while the majority of the rest of Americans enjoyed increasingly fruitful standards of living. President Johnson vowed to end poverty and create increased opportunities for jobs, education, and the enhancement of the quality of life.

Senator Nixon was a major opponent of the Economic Opportunity Act, suggesting that it could lead to inefficiencies and waste as was seen in less broad, local initiatives. Ultimately, the bill was passed by both houses of Congress. Senators passed the bill with 61 yes votes. Republican Senators voted 22-10 against the bill. Democratic Senators voted 72-45 in favor of the bill with Southern Democrats split 11-11.

The House was closer as Republicans voted 145 to 22 against the bill and Democrats voted 204 to 40 in favor. All 144 Northern Democrats voted for the bill while 40 of 100 Southern Democrats voted against it.

## August 20, 1964

*President Johnson signed the Economic Opportunity Act today. Lyndon's war on poverty is certainly a better War than the one he has been fighting in Vietnam. Perhaps this fight will take some of the emphasis off the loss of life in a faraway land and focus the people on increasing the value of life here domestically.*

*As the Senate ultimately adopted the House version of the bill, the process was a good example of the fine art of compromise. As I learned while I was a Senator, criticizing a politician of compromising is ignoring the art of conciliating, balancing and interpreting public opinion. This art is essential to keeping the nation united and enabling the Government to function. Any act of single-handedness only acts to put wedges between and among the branches of government and is only, at best, good for a very short term.*

*Wedges and the division of the branches of government are as harmful as divisiveness is among the American people. To*

33

*succeed, we must all ultimately find common ground that most everyone, while not fully satisfied, can accept. If politicians are anointed with a scepter of power and a maul of separation, it may take significant effort to unwind from such power.*

The 1964 presidential campaign pitted President Johnson against the Republican challenger, Barry Goldwater. Johnson ran on the social policies that he had been tweaking from the Kennedy years. He also was successfully able to demonize Senator Goldwater as being a social conservative extremist, while distracting voters and media stories from the troubles of the War.

Perhaps Johnson's shrewdest set of maneuverings came during the Democratic national convention. His perennial battles with Jack's brother, Robert, may have resulted in an outpouring of backing for Robert to be Johnson's running mate.

The feud between the two men was long-standing. Gasoline was thrown on the fire between the two men when just four years earlier; Robert had tried to block the selection of Johnson as his brother's running mate. Another example was when just hours after his brother was assassinated, Robert received a call from then Vice-president Johnson asking Robert to remind him of the exact words to the Presidential oath of office. The oath of office was perhaps something that Johnson has inherited Attorney General should know, but should not be asked on the heels of the current national and personal crisis.

Robert made President Johnson aware of his desire to become his running mate. To foil that potential likelihood, Johnson set out to see that a convention surge of emotions would not happen. To accomplish this, he managed to schedule Robert's speech for the end of the convention, after the running mate was selected – thus, thwarting any attempt by Attorney General Kennedy to take over the process.

Johnson ended up carrying all but 6 states (all southern) and a whopping 61% of the popular vote.

## November 3, 1964

*Lyndon was elected today. On one hand, I say good for him. I was wondering if his actions with the War would deter too many voters from casting their ballot for him. There are many people who would rather spend money domestically rather than sending our young men to foreign countries where the value to the United States is indirect – if at all.*

*The Nazi aggression in WWII may have taught us a lesson to try to become involved earlier, but we need to be sure that we do not become involved in every act of aggression around the World. While a police force should be respected for the value of providing safety, there is a line that can be crossed. As freedoms are taken away, people may rather be less safe and more free. This is certain for people not under the sovereignty of the United States, but also can be problematic domestically.*

*On the other hand, I am not at all pleased with the way that Lyndon treats Bobby. I admire my brother more than I admire anyone I know. His consistency with his convictions is both a blessing and a curse. A curse when it comes to politics, which often requires a bit of "bending" of your convictions. This curse is good for a leader, but bad for a politician running against individuals who do not hesitate to "break" their convictions for desired outcomes. The more respected coach does not break the rules just to win the game. I do not suppose Bobby would ever put the process ahead of the goal, the means before the end.*

*I am reminded, today, of a conversation that I had with Lyndon... One day on the back porch of the White House, he and I were talking about his future. He very emphatically indicated that he fully intended to run for President after my terms were over. I asked him if he thought he might be too old after my two terms. He paused for a while, and said - "I'll figure something out."*

*He went on to talk about his concern that there was a lot of activity abroad and that all the money and attention we were spending on foreign affairs would detract from all of the social agendas that are in progress and more on the horizon.*

*I am not certain if he was kidding or just thinking from the top of his head, but he made an interesting comment that caused me to pause. He said he intended to create the Great Wall of America and just focus on our own needs and making the people of the United States happy.*

*I reminded him that we all came from immigrants and that our goal was to provide an alternative way of governing that maximized opportunities for all people. We should take in as many people as we can without influencing the welfare of the rest of the country. He cocked his head a bit as if he was processing what I had just said, took a sip of his drink, and chortled, "Damn War!"*

# Chapter 6 – 1965

Three marches from Selma to Montgomery Alabama were orchestrated generally to protest the treatment of blacks in Alabama, one of the last bastions of pervasive prejudicial treatment of blacks in the country.

A march was organized on March 7, 1965 where 500 or so protesters left Selma heading toward Montgomery in an attempt to talk to Governor Wallace about voter rights. Along the way, they were met by a large group of state troopers, many of whom were recently deputized. Perhaps partially due to a lack of training, many of the troopers quickly became violent in their attempt to halt the march, leaving many marchers battered, bloodied, and affected by tear gas – all on television. The exposure by the video images of such a one-sided conflict not only raised awareness of the voter rights cause that was the purpose of the march, but gained an upsurge in backing.

In response to the rise in public sentiment, Dr. Martin Luther King and others organized a second march on the heels of the first. A crowd five times the size of the first march gathered two days later, focusing on overall civil rights in addition to voter rights. There was a court order that did not allow them to march all the way to Montgomery, so when they reached the bridge where the bloody skirmish occurred two days earlier, they prayed, turned around and went back to Selma. While the march was peaceful, several Klu Klux Klan members beat three clergymen, one of whom eventually died.

A week later, a judge lifted the ruling that prevented a march all the way to Montgomery (through Lowndes County) – but limited it to 300, so a third march from Selma to Montgomery was organized on March 21, once again led by Dr. King. All but 300 of the 8,000 marchers camped out after a day of marching, while the others returned to Selma.

For the next two days, marchers headed toward Montgomery County and stopped short of the city for one last camp prior to entering the capital city. By this time, since they were no longer in Lowndes County, they were joined by a flood many other like-minded people. By March 25th, 25,000 people had joined the march and headed to the capital building, where Dr. King addressed the crowd and a petition was eventually handed to a secretary of the governor.

## March 25, 1965

*It is normal for people of the United States, when their freedom is challenged, to peacefully seek a solution that aligns with the country's founding ideals that each citizen has rights and should be afforded equal opportunities, Lincoln, in his Gettysburg address made a point to make certain that everyone understood that 'men' meant 'all men'. In addition, just to be sure, the Civil Rights Act makes sure that 'all men' also means 'all women' and any other aspect that differentiates people.*

*It should be evident to all that the attention that Dr. King has raised on these issues along with the power of the media, has meant that localities around the country, and particularly in the South, can no longer hide behind ignorance of intentions.*

*I applaud Dr. King's efforts and courage and wish him the best in his quest of ensuring all people have the same opportunities to take advantage of what this country has to offer, uninhibited by prejudices that ultimately degrade the high levels of success that all Americans can achieve.*

On July 30, 1965, President Johnson signed into law the social security amendments that resulted in the creation of two keys pieces of the social agenda – Medicaid and Medicare – federal health insurance for the retired and poor. The economy was clicking along fairly well and national sentiment was encouraged by politicians to look inward. This domestic focus was important because the impression of lawmakers was negatively impacted by a very unpopular war in Vietnam.

Once again, President Johnson took advantage of the extremely strong foothold he had in Congress in getting Medicaid and Medicare through the Legislative Branch.

## July 30, 1965

*Today, Lyndon signed a bill, which creates federal health insurance for the elderly and poor. This safety net for two important American populations is an important step to making certain that the opportunities that we as a nation offer are not impeded by health issues that can be treated or prevented.*

*Franklin Roosevelt, when he signed the Social Security Act of 1935 that has since been counted on by a generation was inclined to include health care in the initial bill but was afraid that it would be too much to be passed. Finally, after being discussed for 30 years, it has become law.*

*I tried pushing Medicaid during my election. I was hoping that since I made a strong pitch for it during my debate with Dick Nixon, that it might have had enough political capital to*

39

*be able to be passed early in my term. Unfortunately, I ran into a Republican buzz saw of concern with the cost. My pitch was that if we could run it like an insurance company runs its policies and procedures, that it should be self-sustaining. As long as people are putting into the piggy bank as much or more than they may eventually take out, it should be perpetually solvent. Moreover, with the power of the size of the federal government and a growing number of 'investors', a pot of funding should be able to be maintained.*

*I understand the arguments that the Republicans posed. From when you first start working, your employers are obligated by the federal government to deduct a percentage of your earnings to be held for you as a government-controlled savings account that you draw down from when you retire. It sounds good, you think your money is safe, and you can get yearly statements that tell you how much income you will have when you retire.*

*This sounds like a great system until you start looking under the covers at how politics boils, fries and scrambles your retirement nest egg. Both Republicans and Democrats accuse the other party of being the short order chef that does the boiling, frying and scrambling. Republicans say that Democrats raid the nest and do not leave enough for future generations. Democrats say that Republicans are unwilling to continue to put money into the nest, resulting in not enough for future generations.*

*Both are right and both are wrong. Neither often address the fundamental issue with social security which is that the assumptions today are different that in 1935 when social security was first passed. It is these assumptions that should be addressed every few years as economic and cultural environments influence those assumptions.*

On August 14th, 1965, almost 4,000 national guardsmen had been called to the area of Los Angeles known as Watts. Observers called the situation Vietnam in Los Angeles.

The riots began two days earlier as a young man was pulled over for being suspected for driving while drunk. As officers were processing the traffic violation, they were unaware that apparently the traffic stop happened close to the house where the driver's mother lived. The driver's brother, who was a passenger in the car, walked to the house of the driver's mother to let her know what was going on.

The mother came out to the car and started admonishing her son, the driver, for suspicion of drinking while driving. If is fully unclear as to the actual events that transpired, but the admonishment by the mother somehow led to pushing and shoving and police guns being drawn. These events were all happening in the middle of the Watts area, which was very impoverished and known to have a level of violence and crime.

Because of the news of the traffic violation and perceived police overreaction, riots began. Violence continued through the night as more police officers became involved to try to calm down the community. However, the situation continued to escalate. What started as pent up frustration from life in Watts, turned into an outcry against the poor social conditions and racial challenges that faced the community – and, some would say, the country.

## August 14, 1965

*The riots in Watts over the past couple of days have been very close to home – at least my current home.*

*Violence is not the answer to solving domestic issues. Violence brings attention, but not positive attention. Participants in violence are seen as aggressors and only know one way of solving an issue.*

*Unfortunately, there are situational agitators that use a situation to spark emotions, often emotions that are not at all related to the agenda of the situational agitators. The poverty and challenges in Watts are much broader than the social issues that are being called out as being the catalyst for the violence.*

41

*These situational agitators need to be called out. Their agendas are not necessarily, and often not even close, to addressing the needs of the people. Agitators are, instead, they are using the situation to expand their agenda. Unfortunately, there are social situations that are seen by the social agitators as powder kegs, waiting for the right moment to spark the explosion of emotions that entails. This explosion is the capitalized by the situational agitators to further their agenda.*

On September 9, 1965, President Johnson created the Department of Housing and Urban Development only one month after signing the legislation that provided for its establishment. Housing and Urban Development became a cabinet position.

Some say that President Johnson carried the torch that President Kennedy lit with the words Kennedy spoke at his inauguration. "We dare not forget today that we are the heirs of that first revolution. Let the word go forth from this time and place, to friend and foe alike, that the torch has been passed to a new generation of Americans--born in this century, tempered by war, disciplined by a hard and bitter peace, proud of our ancient heritage--and unwilling to witness or permit the slow undoing of those human rights to which this nation has always been committed, and to which we are committed today at home and around the world."

Others say that Johnson had the legislative power and wherewithal to take liberal ideals and a liberal Congress, capitalize on the giving of the greatest generation, and pass sweeping legislation that would be difficult to unwind.

Regardless of the impetus, the social policies of President Johnson aligned with Kennedy's desire for all Americans to have the opportunity to be contributing members of the society.

## September 10, 1965

*I read today that Johnson created Housing and Urban Development. From what I read of the bill and the scope of what HUD is targeted to accomplish, the new agency should go a long way to create opportunities for Americans to have common footing to achieve the American dream.*

*Achieving the American Dream is easier for some than for others. I am fortunate that I was part of an influential family. Some see that as a silver spoon in my mouth. Let me say that it may have been a silver spoon, but it had brussel sprouts on it. My mother made certain that even though I had the opportunity, I was not going to be spoon-fed the dessert.*

*Then, my experience in World War II convinced me that the Government has a responsibility to be the spoon (maybe not silver), but to not be the sugar. (I heard good things about the movie, so I read the book. Dick Van Dyke and Julie Andrews are two of my favorites.)*

*I was able to take my experiences and turn them into the man that I became. Social programs like Housing and Urban Development are important to provide equal footing, or opportunity to achieve the American Dream, no matter what ultimate goal that dream has for individuals. I am glad that Lyndon was able quickly to establish this important agency.*

President Kennedy did not like the fact that there were quotas on how many people immigrated into the United States and from where. He was very aware that immigrants brought many cultures, creative thinking, and strong passions to the United States, which made the country stronger.

He was so passionate about the topic of immigration that in the late 1950's, he wrote a manuscript that later was transformed into a book "A Nation of Immigrants".

The Immigration Act of 1965 was voted on by the House and Senate with nonpartisan results with 85% of Republicans and

74% of Democrats voting for the bill. Interestingly, one could say that the Republicans were the party of Immigration.

## October 4, 1965

> *I saw Lyndon signing the Immigration bill into law with the Statue of Liberty looming above him. The background was good for television, but the real place that should have been the backdrop for the signatory on this very important piece of legislation would have been Ellis Island, a short boat ride from the statue that oversees in New York harbor.*
>
> *What buildings besides those that sit on Ellis Island better portray the first interaction with America that immigrants had? Moreover, what place in the last one hundred years besides Ellis Island better symbolizes the challenges to enter this country?*
>
> *The melting pot that is the United States is more than just molten iron. Makers of iron know that not enough carbon and the resulting steel that creates county's infrastructure is too weak. Add other elements such as nickel, sulfur, and manganese and the uses of the steel produced from America's melting pot becomes even more strong and flexible.*
>
> *With an immigration policy that is flexible and fair, the needs of both the immigrants and the country can be met. Without that flexibility, we can be locked into quotas that only may make sense on a piece of paper.*

Another chapter in President Johnson's Great Society agenda was a focus on education. When the Higher Education Act was passed, President Johnson chose to go to his alma mater in Texas, Texas State University to sign the bill.

This bill was one of the initial pieces of legislation that took power from the States to educate the people of the States and put the power of the purse for education in the hands of the federal government.

The States were still responsible for funding and administering primary and secondary grades of Kindergarten through twelfth grade, but the federal government was somewhat taking charge of public postsecondary colleges and universities.

While it is difficult to argue with the value in providing financial assistance to high school graduates for their continuing pursuit of education, some saw this as an overreach of federal power.

## November 9, 1965

*Lyndon learned from my error of placing too much emphasis on the denial of federal assistance to educational institutions because of the need to keep church and state separated.*

*As could be predicted, the opposition to the Higher Education Act was focused on whether or not it is right for the federal government even to be involved in the provision of funding to education, which is described in the constitution as being an area for which the States are responsible.*

*Unfortunately, there exists discrepancies from State to State regarding the effectiveness of education, comparing results from one State to the next. The federal government has a role to assist in helping achieve conformity to the educational opportunities of all American children, regardless in what part of the country their parents happen to live. The goal of conformity should not be to bring all children to a middle ground, but rather to set a minimum bar at which all children should achieve and then systematically raise the low bar.*

*The betterment of the children and resulting betterment of the United States hinges on the ability of the educational system to keep the creative and innovative spirit of American youth alive, which keeps the United States at the leading edge to create new, valued products and services for which the entire world benefits.*

# Chapter 7 – 1966

The National Organization of Women was founded on June 30, 1966. It was founded during a meeting of two dozen or so people who were attending a meeting in Washington, D.C. of the National Conference of State Commissions on the Status of Women.

The President's Commission on the Status of Women was established by President Kennedy during his shortened term in office. Discrimination against women was very much in line with the President's focus on the elimination of discrimination in all societal aspects where policies based on differences can be made. Obviously, gender is a major source of potential discrimination and theoretically could affect half of the population.

Kennedy's first chairperson of this commission was Eleanor Roosevelt.

The National Organization of Women took their initial charge to be the enforcement of the Civil Rights Act of 1964 and the discrimination outlined in that act. They expanded the ways discrimination could be viewed to include gender and to attempt to broaden women's choices.

At first the National Organization of Women were seen as a group of women that did not want children, did not want to worry about decorating or cleaning the house, or did not want to cook.

The organizers of this organization sought to expand the perception of their role to, at a minimum, receiving acknowledgement that women should not be pigeonholed into wife-type stereotypes. Instead, they pushed the pendulum to the opposite side, encouraging all women to burn their aprons, mops and bras and do what men do.

## June 30, 1966

*It is clear that women should have equal opportunities as men have. The federal government can certainly help clear the paths for women to feel as though they have the ability to make all the choices that men do.*

*These opportunities should be applied to the variety of decisions that United States citizens make – where to live, who to vote for, what career to pursue, where to receive higher education, and how to spend leisure time.*

*The biggest barrier is to change the perception of anyone who attempts to hang on to a culture of pigeonholing women into specific roles or expectations. To say that a woman is in charge of cooking is setting up a barrier that may be difficult to overcome. If the woman chooses to be in charge of cooking or a discussion in dividing household functions results in an agreement that the woman will be the chief cook, then the role or expectation has been equally set.*

*If the man states that the women's job is to cook without regard to her wishes or thoughts about what household roles she wishes to take on, then the pigeonholing culture has not been addressed.*

*Just as destructive to the ability of the woman to escape the barriers of opportunities to choose is to coerce a woman to engage in activities, decisions or follow opportunities because they are expressly NOT in the mainstream way of thinking.*

*Women (or men) should not be made to feel bad about decisions or choices that they make just because they do not conform to someone else's way of thinking. This should apply to all social questions not matter on which side of the argument they fall.*

*Government should give everyone the opportunity to access the vegetable field, but not stand in the way or take sides in the selection of vegetables to pick.*

President Johnson was very reluctant to sign the Freedom of Information Act in to law. He felt as though there was government information that should be kept secret as sensitive pieces of information.

Proponents of the legislation felt that the Government WAS the people and that the people should know everything that the Government was doing. The idea was that it would be difficult for government entities to be corrupt if they are transparent.

Unlike most other bills passed by Congress, this one was very short – two pages. Arguable, it was readable by all members of Congress in a day or two. It was signed into law in 1966 on Independence Day and was made to be effective exactly a year later in 1967.

Many terms were coined or more frequently used after this bill was mainstreamed. The definitions provided are not the Webster versions, but rather definitions that have evolved in some circles.

**Redacted** – the document is released, but all the information that can tell you what the document means is covered by black lines

**Declassified** – Enough time has passed that there is no longer any political reason to keep it secret

**Discretional Release** – the government releases information even though they do not have to

**Retroactive Classification** – the government can (even though they did not think that it was initially important), once someone has expressed interest in information, retroactively make it classified so it cannot be disclosed

## July 5, 1966

*Transparency is a hallmark of any government that is interested in the establishing and maintaining the trust of the citizens. The Freedom of Information Act is a good example of an attempt to provide easy and comprehensive access to information to maintain transparency.*

*It is unfortunate that the government cannot be self-regulated and transparent without a new law. Nevertheless, as government gets larger, it supports more facets of daily living and there are more people that feel as if there is information that is not necessary to divulge and is best kept from the public.*

*The growth of government is inevitable, more than just because the population grows, but because there becomes a greater call for States to become more homogenous as information about the positives and negatives of life around the United States becomes better known.*

*The child who receives the equivalent of a deck of playing cards or new boots for his birthday is satisfied with his gifts until he begins to realize that his friends are getting a lot more. At that point, he has at least two choices. One choice is to make certain he does well in school, gets a good job and can afford more than boots for his birthday. Another choice is to complain to his parents that he should be entitled to more because his friends get more.*

*We should do all we can to promote the first choice, rather than the second. I imagine that a nation that collectively is focused more on what government can provide to them is a nation that will become less able to better and provide for them.*

*I would tell the child, "Ask not what your parents can do for you, ask what you can do for your parents – or yourself."*

In 1966, there was a lot of pressure on politicians to address the increase in deaths on the highways of America. Cars were getting faster and the highways were not necessarily keeping up with the increased speeds. In a 40-year period leading up to this legislation, deaths on the roads had increased by six times.

The National Traffic and Motor Vehicle Safety Act was the response of Congress to this issue. It gave the Federal government the right set rules and regulations for motor vehicles and the roads on which they travel and to attempt to affect changes in driver behavior.

Safety measures sought to increase the safety of vehicles by improving windshields, steering wheels and adding safety belts. No longer was the mother's quick, stiff right arm extension a safety feature of driving.

Safety on the roads was initially improved by better signage, markings on the road, barriers, and guardrails.

Driver behavior was enhanced through education and enforcement of safety laws.

The result of these measures saw a quick and marked improvement in the numbers of traffic deaths and damage to vehicles and property.

## September 10, 1966

*As new technologies are developed, there are greater possible needs for legislation that controls the technologies. Yesterday's passage of the National Traffic and Motor Vehicle Safety Act is another example of one of these types of laws.*

*It is not difficult to see why motor vehicle safety is important, not only to protect the lives of the driver and passengers, but also to protect the lives of everyone else on the road. The behavior of an individual is his or her own business unless it impinges on the freedoms of fellow citizens.*

*If a man builds a car that is four wheels and an engine on top of a gigantic gas tank that can be ignited with a random spark, it is the duty of the government to make certain that this man's car is not allowed on public roads. He can blow himself up driving on his own property, but a family of five driving to Florida on vacation should not have to worry about his exploding car interfering with their plans.*

*I assume my driver's license has expired.*

# Chapter 8 – 1967

On January 3, 1967, Jacob Leon Rubenstein died. A little over three years after killing Lee Harvey Oswald, Jack Ruby died of an embolism associated with lung cancer just as his retrial for Oswald's death was being arranged.

### January 4, 1967

*It may seem a bit callous, but I am pleased that the public spectacle of a retrial for Jack Ruby did not need to be endured by my family or the people of the United States.*

The first super bowl was held on January 15, 1967 pitting the Green Bay Packers against the Kansas City chiefs. Green Bay ended up winning 35-10.

The National Football League decided it was losing ground by competing with the upstart American Football League. Therefore, in 1966 they started talking about a merger. The merger kept the two separate, but equal. For the first championship game where the winners of both leagues played each other, there was a bit of rivalry to prove which league was better. The older National Football League was satisfied with their win and, in their minds; this initial game resulted in the establishment of the National Football League at the best organization.

## January 16, 1967

*Los Angeles played host to the AFL-NFL World Championship game at the Los Angeles coliseum yesterday. Maybe one of these days they will let me venture out and watch some football in person. At least, though, it was televised. It is not at all like our backyard games at Martha's Vineyard.*

*I had a bet with Frank. I picked Green Bay. I am not complaining about the treatment that I receive here, but sometime in the next year, he now must figure out how to take me to a restaurant!*

The Twenty-fifth Amendment to the Constitution was ratified on February 23, 1967. The original language of the constitution discusses the succession plans for the President, but is not specific enough to avoid interpretation. The Twenty-fifth Amendment adds clarity to the Presidential succession if the President can no longer pursue his or her duties as President. The Constitutional Amendment also addresses the situation where a President is disabled.

The succession confusion began as far back as 1841 when President William Harrison was the first President to die in office. President Harrison died soon after getting sick after his inaugural speech, which was outdoors, and in very bad weather. He got sick and died of pneumonia after only one month in office.

After President Harrison's death, there were suggestions that the Vice President, John Tyler, should take over as Acting President until a new President could be elected. Tyler ignored these suppositions, taking over the post in an official capacity and not acting, becoming the tenth President of the United States.

Another disability occurred when President Wilson suffered a stroke while in office.  His wife all but took over for him, assuming his daily tasks as President until he left office in March of 1921, the end of his term.

The Kennedy shooting forced Congress to act because they were concerned that the United States needed a leader to quickly and seamlessly be in place in case of national emergency.

On February 10, 1967, Nevada became the final State needed to ratify the Amendment.  It was formally signed into adoption three days later.

## February 24, 1967

*I was just reading some details about the 25th Amendment that was finally ratified by Nevada a couple weeks ago and signed into adoption.*

*The issue of political succession got me thinking about my situation, and I asked Frank if he knew whether Lyndon had a body double.  He said that he assumed that he did, but it likely took several months before someone was found and trained to be able to take over as my Presidential decoy apparently was.  He also speculated that Lyndon would not be taking many chances with public appearances.  I chuckled to myself and agreed.*

*I then asked if he knew what Lyndon's reaction was when he was told about the decoy program. Frank said that until one is needed, the President does not know that the program exists.  This made sense because I did not know until just before the trip to Dallas.*

*Frank went on to say that the other safeguard that he thought they would use if they needed to, was to tell Lyndon that the program was brand new so he would not be aware of my existence.  I thought that was good, because the last thing Lyndon needs is to think that I may pop in out of nowhere and try to take my job back.  This time I chuckled aloud.*

About five months after Congress passed a bill authorizing its establishment; the United States Department of Transportation was operational on April 1, 1967. Establishing the Department of Transportation as a cabinet position was initially suggested to President Johnson in 1965 and two years later was seen to fruition.

The last thirty years in the twentieth century saw a large growth in the size of the Presidential cabinet, greater even than the growth of government. As of the beginning of 2014, there were fifteen cabinet positions and eight cabinet level officers for twenty-three positions. The fifteen cabinet positions and when they were established include: Secretary of State (1789), Secretary of Treasury (1789), Secretary of Defense (1949 – was Secretary of War in 1789), Attorney General (1789), Secretary of the Interior (1849), Secretary of Agriculture (1889), Secretary of Commerce (1913), Secretary of Labor (1913), Secretary of Health and Human Services (1953), Secretary of Housing and Urban Development (1966), Secretary of Transportation (1967), Secretary of Energy (1977), Secretary of Education (1979), Secretary of Veterans Affairs (1989), and Secretary of Homeland Security (2003).

Cabinet-level officers include Vice President, White House Chief of Staff, Director of the Office of Management and Budget. Administrator of the Environmental Protection Agency, Trade Representative, Ambassador to the United Nations, Chairperson of the Council of Economic Advisers, and Administrator of the Small Business Administration.

The following chart (Figure 1) graphs the increase in the size of the cabinet since established in 1789.

Figure 1

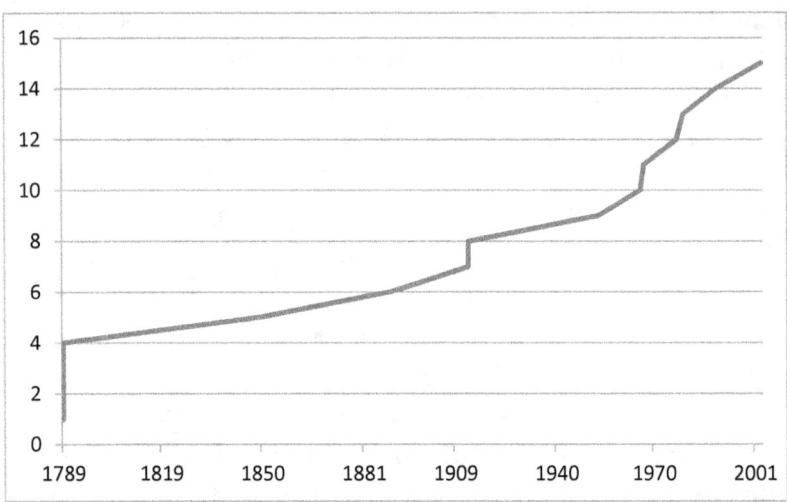

As a comparison, the following chart (Figure 2) graphs government spending.

Figure 2

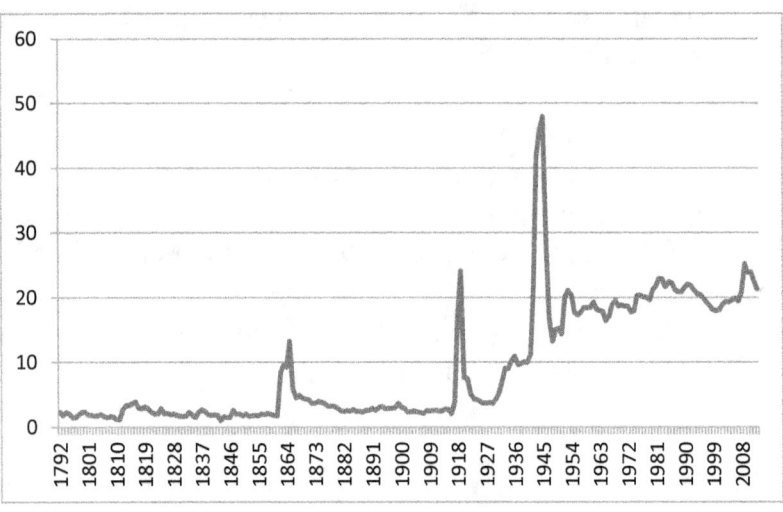

# April 2, 1967

*I read where a new cabinet post was created to pay attention to transportation.*

*The Presidential cabinet is an interesting group. While I enjoyed working with each member of my cabinet and appreciated their input into decisions, the body of a cabinet that meets regularly is not terribly useful. Only in certain circumstances, when there is overlap among multiple areas of government covered by multiple cabinet positions would it be useful to talk to more than one at a time. The exception may be if the President has a high-level set of policies that need to be rolled out and a single set of messages delivered.*

*As the Presidential cabinet grows, it appears that government is growing, which in a sense it is. However, the reality of the size of the cabinet is more proportional to the complexity of society.*

*When the Presidential cabinet was first formed, there were four posts – Secretaries of State, Treasury, War, and the Attorney General. Nevertheless, life and society was relatively simple in the 1700's. We needed to protect ourselves from foreign invasions (State and War), from ourselves (Attorney General) and a method to pay for it all (Treasury).*

*Fifty years later, there was a need for a greater focus on how land was managed – government land and land available for the public to settle on. Thus, the Secretary of Interior was established. Twenty-four years after that, more people were buying and selling goods and the Department of Interior was created.*

*The complexities and multiple dimensions of society made it more difficult for the President to know everything that is going on, even at a high level. The cabinet provides advice and helps to administer Presidential policy and laws created by Congress, who, by the way, no longer only works in December.*

## May 28, 1967

*I saw that yesterday Jackie and Caroline attended the christening of the new Navy carrier, the John F. Kennedy. It is flattering to have a carrier named after you, when all you could manage to skipper was a PT boat. I think the last thing on my crew's mind was whether they could follow me to a bigger ship. We were in the middle of the Pacific Ocean in a boat that, while was engineered well to accomplish its purpose, could hardly get out of its shadow in competition with some other vessels. We made the best in our situation, thanks to an excellent crew who tried hard to understand a guy who sounded like he stepped on the boat straight from a street in Boston. When the responses to my accent came back in Cajun, I always chuckled.*

*The pictures of the new carrier are impressive.*

Loving v. Virginia was a Supreme Court decision that held up the legality of interracial marriages and made laws scattered throughout the United States, particularly the South, unconstitutional. The Supreme Court decision was made public on June 12, 1967.

The case of Mildred and Richard Loving came before the Supreme Court as they each had been sentenced to a year in Virginia prison for violating the Virginia law of a white person marrying a colored person. The Supreme Court found in favor of the Lovings, overturning a Supreme Court decision in 1883, which upheld Alabama's prohibition of interracial marriages.

Justice Warren's opinion included a statement that equated marriage as a fundamental civil right. The Justice included the Fourteenth Amendment as the legal backing of the unanimous decision. It was a freedom that could not be taken away by the government.

The apropos, Loving Day, is celebrated on the anniversary of the Supreme Court's decision – June 12th.

# June 13, 1967

*Choosing who you want to marry is a freedom that everyone should have. It is no surprise that the Supreme Court was unanimous in its decision that interracial marriages must be legal and laws against these types of marriages declared unconstitutional.*

*I feel bad that the Lovings had to be subject to being behind bars for following their hearts and not a law that never should have been on the books in the first place.*

*Prejudices are a difficult thing to manage. We all may have prejudices of some sort or another. It seems as though prejudices are human nature at their core, but in many cases, they are simply someone who is saying, "I like myself so much and what I am. So much, that I do not like you."*

*Some "thin" people are prejudiced against "thick" people. Maybe they worked hard to lose weight to be thin and now cannot see why everyone else should not be that way. In the process of losing weight, they have developed a passion for watching what they eat and are proud that they were successful. So, rather than putting themselves in someone else's shoes and showing empathy, they exhibit prejudicial behaviors.*

*Some "smarter" people are prejudiced against "less smart" people. Some think that if you are not educated in a particular area, that you are lesser of a person. Other smarter people may be prejudiced against you because of the college that you attended. Why should discovering a cure for the common cold at a small college in Indiana be less "smart" than a law degree at Harvard? Trust me; I have seen some of the people that have graduated from an Ivy League school. In a very eloquent Bostonian voice, I can still hear a ringing in my ear, "Which end of this shoe horn goes in my shoe."*

*We need to not only recognize our differences, but also understand that someone who may seem to be different is not. Our message against prejudice is muddied when we fight against*

*it in one societal area, and then turn around and behave
prejudicial in another.*

*The quick glance at someone who is obviously opposite of
how we perceive ourselves is not the time to pre judge, but to
embrace.*

## August 12, 1967

*Finally, Frank paid off his bet and we ventured out to a
restaurant. It was about 20 minutes from the bunker, and we took
a couple vehicles to get there.*

*My guardians put a disguise on me, which I thought was
very good and commented on its realism to Frank. He said, "Yes,
Mr. President, is looks good, but do me a favor, please don't talk in
public. We can't do anything about the fact that you still sound
like you."*

*The restaurant was very nice, likely one of the better
restaurants in the Los Angeles area. We did not sit in the main
dining area. Instead, we quickly scampered off to a private room.
I followed directions, the only time I spoke outside our small group
of four, in a room for about ten, was with the waitress. We went
around the table and told her our order. When she got to me, and I
order the Salmon special, she paused and turned her head as if she
recognized the voice, but could not place the face.*

*The waitress asked, "Have we met? Have you been here
before?" I told her that I did not think so. Frank was noticeably
fidgeting. She seemed satisfied and left to put our orders in.
Frank said, "You see, Mr. President, why I asked you not to talk.
People still remember your voice. It is on television regularly.
She was likely in her early teens or maybe younger when you were
in the White House." I am not certain I appreciated Frank's
comment about my age, but I am certain it was with good
intentions.*

*Frank ordered a bottle of wine. I do not recall the
vineyard, but noticed that it was from Napa Valley. California has*

*certainly come a long way with American wines. It is nice not to have to import all of our grape products. Perhaps one day we will be exporting wine to Spain and France instead of importing it all.*

*Our dinners came and the Salmon was excellent. There was a taste of rosemary and a sprig of rosemary garnish. I had forgotten that very distinctive fragrance. I asked Frank if we could acquire some herb plants for the bunker. I thought the smells might be a nice change of pace and looked forward to watching them grow. The rosemary reminded me of my poor, but strong sister.*

*We finished our dinner and exited out the back door of the restaurant, I knew Frank was doing his job, but it took a little away from the experience for which I was hoping.*

*We returned to the bunker safe and sound. Frank looked exhausted, I knew he was nervous about the excursion, but he did not let it show until we returned. He is a consummate professional.*


Thurgood Marshall moved up the ranks of court justices with an appointment by President Kennedy in 1961 as Second Circuit United States Court of Appeals judge. Justice Marshall gained notoriety as a lawyer who frequently argued in front of the Supreme Court, earning him respect and credentials to serve as an appellate juror.

President Johnson gave Justice Marshall a promotion with a 1965 appointment to the post of Solicitor General. Two years later, Marshall continued his fast track and was nominated by President Johnson to the Supreme Court, confirmed by the Senate with over two thirds of the vote.

Justice Marshall was sworn in on October 10, 1967, becoming the first African American justice on the Supreme Court and proceeded to serve in that position for twenty-four years.

## October 15, 1967

*Congratulations, Justice Marshall on your historic appointment to the Supreme Court. Your story is testament to someone who achieved a goal not because of the color of his skin, but because of hard work and determination.*

*Often, opportunity is not as available for some as it is for others. My opportunity was certainly a different opportunity than Justice Marshall had and our roads were miles apart. However, what we may have in common is an ability to make the best of the opportunities that are presented to us.*

*Not all opportunities can, or should be the same. We all have different passions that take us down different paths. When I was a small boy, I did not think much about being on a boat in the Navy during a worldwide war. My life took that path. I made the best of that time, learned from it, and perhaps history will show that I applied some of what I learned in future decisions that I made.*

*I look for the day when the color of a man or woman's skin is not even a factor when choosing a representative to political office or to a court. It should not be a factor in choosing, or not choosing, the best candidate.*

# Chapter 9 – 1968

On April 4, 1968, Dr. Martin Luther King was assassinated while standing on a second floor balcony at the Lorraine Motel in Memphis Tennessee. The shooter, James Earl Ray, was across the street at a boarding house. Ray was not captured for two months, finally being held in London as he attempted to leave the country. He died in prison thirty years later.

Subsequent to the shooting, race riots broke out despite many leaders' attempts to quell the violence. Dr. King's continual message of change through peaceful demonstration was the antithesis of the violent war cry of justice for his killing.

Robert Kennedy was campaigning in Indianapolis on the day Dr. King was shot. Kennedy attempted to make sense out of the senseless act of the shooting. Early in Kennedy's remarks, he attempted to capitalize on the ongoing sentiment of Dr. King when he said, "replace that violence, that stain of bloodshed that has spread across our land, with an effort to understand with compassion and love."

One of Kennedy's most memorable excerpts from his speech was, "What we need in the United States is not division, what we need in the United States is not hatred, what we need in the United States is not violence or lawlessness, but love and wisdom, and compassion toward one another, and a feeling of justice towards those who still suffer within our country, whether they be white or whether they be black."

## April 5, 1968

*Unfortunately, Dr. King practically predicted his fate yesterday in Memphis. He made little attempt to protect himself, not because he wanted to be a martyr, but because he felt and wanted to show that he was with the people, not above them. Dr. King's desire to pursue peacefully equal opportunities should not have been a difficult request to fulfil.*

*I hope that America takes note of Dr. King's message and not apply his skin color as a filter to that message. Politicians on both sides of the aisle need to take note. I read Bobby's speech in Indianapolis in response to the killing of Dr. King. I wish I was there. I am proud of my brother.*

*Bobby's message of justice over prejudice and compassion over violence is an excellent summary of Dr. King's wishes and the wishes of anyone who truly believes that ALL are created equal.*

On June 4, 1968, Robert Kennedy had learned that his campaigning for President was showing strength, some said enough strength to make a run at the Democratic nomination, particularly with President Johnson pulling his hat out of the running. Kennedy had recently won the support of California and South Dakota and on his way to what may be a very interesting Democratic Convention.

Kennedy was staying at the Ambassador Hotel in Los Angeles where he had been actively campaigning on primary day.

Shortly after midnight, rather than meeting a smaller group of supporters after addressing a crowd gathered at the hotel's ballroom, Kennedy was escorted through the hotel's kitchen to conduct a quickly formed press conference.

Sirhan Sirhan either was "fortunate" or somehow knew that Kennedy would be walking by his position in the hotel's kitchen. As Kennedy quickly walked by on his was to talk to the press regarding his recent campaign success, Sirhan Sirhan shot Kennedy multiple times, including what ended up being a fatal shot to the head at point blank range.

Kennedy was transferred to nearby Good Samaritan hospital where a team of doctors worked to try to save his life for about twenty-four hours. Just before two o'clock in the morning of June 6, 1968, the twenty-two caliber bullet that splintered inside his head, killed the younger brother of President Kennedy.

Notes found in the killer's residence and a newspaper article found in his pocket provided a direct relationship to Robert Kennedy's support of Israel in the Israeli/Palestinian conflict. The initial assumptions that the assassination was related to Kennedy's support of the civil rights movement were dashed by these artifacts.

In hindsight, if the rationale for the killing was seeped in a response to the Israeli/Palestinian conflict, this assassination could be the first significant example of domestic terrorism on United States soil.

Following Robert Kennedy's assassination, President Johnson issued an executive order for the Secret Service to begin immediately protecting presidential candidates. This order was obviously too late for Bobby, but a necessary step for the future protection of candidates.

Had Bobby continued to mount a strong contention for President and been successful in his bid for the Democratic nomination at the convention in Chicago, he may have been the second Kennedy to win a Presidential election from Republican nominee Richard Nixon.

# June 6, 1968

*Bobby, I wish you would have taken what happened to me and be more careful. Instead, you did the opposite and put yourself out there further, becoming a target – and so close to where I am currently living.*

*It was not surprising that your opinions and ideals took had the impact they had. You were always more idealistic than the rest of the family. I admired that. You did not waiver, nor let anything sway you from those ideals. Even if they were not popular.*

*I only wish you had an opportunity to sit in the chair I used to sit in. You would have been an excellent President. Better than I was. Your focus on human rights was unmatched by everyone except maybe Dr. King.*

*I remember the day we spent the afternoon on the porch outside the Oval Office. After a few stiff drinks and wonderful Washington weather, we were waxing poetic. The most interesting discussion we had was when we were talking about whom you would have as your running mate. I applauded your desire to have Dr. King as your Vice President selection, I am just not certain the country would have been ready for it. I argued that it might have given the Republicans a leg up, as they would have likely won the Southern Democrats over no matter whom they ran against you - even Dick Nixon. However, I knew your idealism and stubbornness would have prevailed.*

*You reminded me of my choice. As we chatted, I agreed that all things being equal, I should have chosen someone else. The account that I read about Lyndon calling you from Air Force One to remind him of the exact wording of the Presidential Oath of Office infuriated me. I knew right away that he did that on purpose to get under your skin, which I am sure he succeeded in doing.*

*What I did not hear much about, was whether you were involved in looking into his involvement in the shooting that*

*November. It all seemed too coincidental. Had it been in any other State, I may have been less confident that there was a possibility of his involvement. Not only that, but I never got a chance to tell you. Lyndon finally talked me into the open convertible. He contended that we needed the vote of the South to get our agenda to move through Congress quickly and the openness and approachability of the convertible would help Southern citizens and politicians be swayed to our side. I have thought about those days many times.*

*Sorry I was not there for you longer, Bobby. I do not know that I could have prevented what happened to you, but I certainly would have tried.*

The Democratic National Convention in Chicago was held at a time when the war in Vietnam was peaking and at the same time that protests against the war were also at a high. Despite Mayor Daley's efforts to maintain law and order during the convention, it became a magnet for protesters from all over the country. For months before the convention, Chicago city police, at the direction of the mayor, prepared for what they believed may be riots in the streets. Mayor Daley knew that keeping the city safe would be important to the city and to him politically.

Part of Mayor Daley's preparation was to equip the police with not only their normal guns and billy clubs, but he also made certain they had mace, riot helmets and other riot gear to keep them safe. His goal was to ensure that his police force would be able to maintain control of any situation that may face them. He knew the eyes of the world, the nation, and Chicago voters would be on his handling of the event.

Protesters gathered by the droves in Chicago as anticipated. For the most part, they were peaceful. At least, peaceful is the way they intended and all started. Most of the protesters wanted to be consistent in their approach to protests - just as adamant, they were that violence in the Vietnam War, and they did not want to protest violence with violence. Peace was the solution to both.

The Mayor's office attempted to use permitting as a way to control protests. This was a good idea, but may have flared anger in the attempt to control protesters' freedom of speech. The Mayor's office did all they could to prevent gatherings by limiting, stonewalling and denying applications for permits to gather in protest of the war.

Therefore, protesters were being told that they cannot legally assemble and they were watching police become geared up for a fight with their riot gear. This caused some of the protesters to morph from peace to aggression. The morphing was further triggered by a shooting that occurred on the Thursday of the weekend before the convention with the killing of a seventeen-year-old boy by police. The boy was out past curfew, approached by police officers, drew a gun, tried to shoot at police but the gun misfired. Police immediately fired back and killed the boy.

The next day, on Friday, protesters were assembling without a permit and some were arrested.

On Saturday, there were more arrests for assembling after curfew, emotions were raised and rocks were thrown at police cars.

On Sunday, a music concert was being planned. Police were attempting to prevent the concert from happening. By the time police agreed to let the concert proceed, word had gotten around that police were still being obstructionists. A small riot broke out as this fueled the violent emotions from the past few days.

The rest of the week (the last week in August 1968) continued similarly to the way the protester / police interactions started on Sunday. The perimeter around the convention center was eventually turned into a picture that could have been from World War II.

## August 29, 1968

*The methods that the Democratic Party members address social issues sometimes make them a lightning rod for demonstrators. When you reach out and try to make everyone happy, you are certain not to succeed because there are often two sides to every issue. One side will be happy with your rhetoric and the other side may be angry that you are not speaking to them.*

*As technology allows everything you say to be recorded and by the next day be broadcast, the opportunity for them to use your words against you with the opposite view is high.*

*As we deal with both sides of the coin, we need to make certain that we treat both sides fairly and respond to issues based on the merits of each position. It is similar to the person who is training to be an Olympic athlete. One of the concepts of weight lifting is to strengthen both sides of the movement. For example, if you are strengthening the muscles in your chest, it is just as important to strengthen the muscles in your back. This maintains posture and helps prevent injuries that could be caused by poor posture or the muscles in front pulling too hard on the back. The Olympic athlete understands this principle and makes certain that opposing muscles are equally strengthened.*

*It is a bit of a play on words, but political movements must be as balanced as athletic movements are. If the population is split fifty-fifty regarding their opinions on a particular issue, then taking one side at the detriment of the other only results in atrophy of support by the side that is not receiving any attention. The wise strategist finds a way to offer enough emphasis on both sides to make each strong enough to maximize success and balance.*

*The sloppy and somewhat lazy strategist only focused on one side. The result can be something that looks like the Hunchback of Notre Dame.*

President Johnson signed The Gun Control Act of 1968 into law on October 22, 1968. This law marked an increased control over gun owners and gun sellers. With the interstate commerce law providing cover, President Johnson continued his focus on his "Great Society" social engineering plans. The recent assassinations of Robert Kennedy and Martin Luther King Jr. provided easing of the volume of the voices of detractors and an opportunity to stretch the control legislation more than otherwise would have been feasible.

The law focused on eliminating sales of firearms to criminals, including convictions for drug offenses, illegal aliens, people who have been dishonorably discharged from the armed forces, people who are "mentally defective", people who have renounced their United Stated citizenship, people who are subject to a domestic violence restraint order or people who have been convicted of domestic violence.

It was a big day for newspaper headlines because also on October 22nd, Shirley Chisholm of New York became the first African-American woman elected to Congress. Later, in 1972, Congresswoman Chisholm became the first woman to run for the Democratic nomination for President of the United States. She would have been the first woman from either political party had Senator Margaret Chase Smith not run for the Republican nomination eight years earlier in 1964.

## October 23, 1968

*Owning guns is not only a right afforded to Americans by the Constitution, but also it helps provide people with security when they feel as though they need to take security in their own hands. This feeling will likely not diminish unless there is a way to guarantee everyone's security, which is a difficult, if not impossible, promise to make. Government can assist in attempting to keep firearms out of the hands of nefarious people, but determining who is capable of arbitrarily taking another's life cannot be predicted.*

*The challenge is to maintain freedoms for gun owners and balance that freedom with the rights of citizens not to be randomly shot at. Too much in one direction and either firearm usage is not controlled and people fear for their safety or people feel as though control over their one's own security is being compromised.*

*If legislation is passed that only addresses of these sides of the pendulum, then many people are alienated. Even though Congress often seems tedious and slow to accomplish anything, that deliberate speed by which it moves is often beneficial in making certain both sides are heard and solutions can be formed that do not fall too far on one side or the other. The lack of the checks between each can lead to a dictatorial feeling by the people, which may lead to some level of revolt. Although, much of the revolting that I have seen in the television would involve flowers, women in long skirts, and a Volkswagen microbus with a coat of paint that certainly was not there when it left the assembly plant.*

*In addition, I saw where Ms. Chisholm became the first black woman to be elected to Congress. She seems to be a very strong woman. While I cannot fully empathize, I fully respect her for being the first black woman to reach this height of political office. I can only imagine the barriers that she has had to overcome to get where she is and the barriers that she is certain to face as she maneuvers the Congress of the United States. I am interested to follow her political career and see how she continues to meet her goals.*

Following the assassination of her brother-in-law, Robert Kennedy, Jackie Kennedy decided that the United States might not be the best place to live for her safety and, more importantly, the safety of her children.

Then, what some called a marriage of convenience, four months after Bobby's death, she married Aristotle Socrates Onassis. Onassis was able to continue a lifestyle that Jackie was used to without her having to worry about asking for help from the Kennedy trust fund. Onassis had a private island home, Skorpios, where they were married, a huge yacht named Christine after Onassis' daughter, a house in Athens and an apartment in Paris.

The wedding cut Jackie's official ties to the United States government, as she was no longer a "widow" of a United States President, so she lost protection from the Secret Service and her ability to send mail without charge (which the United States Postal Service calls a franking privilege – something that is less valuable with email).

## October 29, 1968

*I definitely understand why Jackie decided to remarry. However, I am a bit surprised it took her so long. There are two things she was likely looking for - safety and security. What she went through in November of 1963 was more that someone should have to endure. In her mind, whatever caused the shooting then, could repeat against the family. In addition, she needed someone who had enough money that could keep her lifestyle similar or better than what she was used to. Not that she is inordinately focused on glamour and limelight, just the contrary. After all, it is hard to exceed being First Lady of the United States.*

*Onassis seems like a good gentleman. He offers her protection and a measure of isolation since he has his own island. He certainly has enough money to support her, whatever she wants or needs. In addition, just as important, she will be able to keep the children safe. The Kennedy family sometimes does not seem to have a lot of luck. Of course, perhaps Dad's legacy of running a bit fast and loose rubs off. His children are in his image.*

*Oh, to go back to the days where Jackie and I did not have all the pressures of high political offices. Of course, both of us knew there was some destiny involved, but did not realize the speed to get to that destiny and toll it would take. I still am convinced, the pressures led to the challenges we had having children. I am rambling. Thank you Jackie for the years we had. I appreciate you keeping Caroline and John safe and continuing to raise them as good people. Good luck with your new life.*

Some say that the election of 1968 was a swing of the pendulum away from the close to four decades of New Deal and

Great Society socialistic policies. Just four years earlier, President Johnson had won a landslide victory and was set to run successfully for a second term. Between the Vietnam War and moderating pressures, President Johnson decided not to run and left the door open for his Vice President, Hubert Humphrey.

Johnson's address to the nation after the New Hampshire primary was seen by many as a selfless act of wanting to get a job done that he had promised to do – end the Vietnam War. His speech concluded with the surprise announcement, "With America's sons in the field far away, with America's future under challenge right here at home, with our hopes and the world's hopes for peace in the balance every day, I do not believe that I should devote an hour or a day of my time to any personal partisan causes or to any duties other than the awesome duties of this office – the presidency of your country. Accordingly, I shall not seek, and I will not accept the nomination of my party for another term as your President." While many were surprised by his announcement, those close to the inner circle believed it was inevitable.

Another Democrat, Georgia Governor George Wallace, was less focused on federal intervention in the Southern States and had a great deal of popularity in the South, particularly in Georgia, Alabama, Mississippi, Louisiana and Arkansas. Since, although working hard on the campaign trail to garner support, he could not get the Democratic nomination over Humphrey, he decided to run as an Independent.

Nixon was able to gather 31.7 million popular votes (43.4%), a half million more than Humphrey was. However, Governor Wallace may have seriously weakened Humphrey's chances to win the election. Adding only fifty-five percent of Governor Wallace's votes to Vice President Humphrey's, he would have won the popular vote.

# November 6, 1968

*Dick finally was elected President. I think he may have been working toward this goal his entire career. Even though we were opponents, overall he is a good guy. He is good at surrounding himself with the right people and always seems to get out of jams well. I hear that he is going to rely on Kissinger for foreign affairs. Excellent choice. Henry is probably the best person for that role given the current foreign relationship environment, whether the President is Democrat or Republican.*

*I remember meeting Dick for dinner one evening near the Capital before we had to stop talking because we were running against each other. We had a lively debate about capital punishment. Dick maintained that capital punishment was necessary as a deterrent. I maintained that capital punishment was not a deterrent because it was too easy to be acquitted, find a loophole, or plea down to a lesser charge. In any case, it takes so long to try the cases, get to a disposition and then go through the appellate process that any criminal that may even think in the back of his mind that he may 'get the chair' for doing what he is doing is going to discount it because of the odds of the death penalty actually being carried out.*

*Dick was quoting statistics about recidivism and crime in States that enforced capital punishment. I pushed back and grinned as he was spewing forth his facts and statistics. Finally, he noticed that I had tuned him out and stopped what seemed to be his debate practicing. He asked why I was grinning. I told him that it was difficult to pay attention to him. He asked why, and I said that all I could do was watch the beads of sweat form as he got more and more focused on his point. He pouted the rest of the dinner.*

# Chapter 10 – 1969

The gay liberation movement is often said to have begun in June of 1969 at the Stonewall Inn in New York City. The Stonewall Inn was in the Greenwich Village section of Manhattan. In 1969, The Stonewall Inn was known to be a gathering place for people who did not fit into societal norms. Police raids were routine as gay behavior was discouraged and, in many areas, illegal.

In the early hours of June 28, 1969, the police performed what they thought would be one of the typical raids that they had been somewhat regularly conducting. However, on this day, the patrons were not as compliant as they usually were and a skirmish turned into a riot.

Tempers did not subside as protests and additional skirmishes between the gay population and police in the Greenwich Village area were regular occurrences over the next days and weeks. This was not the last time that police in New York City had negative interactions with the gay community, but many say marked the beginning of the gay movement.

## June 30, 1969

*While I do not pretend to fully understand the lifestyle of members of the gay community because it is different from what I was taught or experienced, I believe that the people who live that lifestyle should not be discriminated against. Gay lifestyles should be protected just as gender, race and religion is protected. Period. Just because we do not understand, or cannot relate to a particular lifestyle does not mean that it is wrong.*

*People who are gay should have the right to live their lives as they choose providing their behaviors do not infringe on the rights of others to live their lives as they see fit. On the obverse, people, who because of religious practices and convictions, should not be forced to believe that those behaviors are part of their beliefs. Acceptance of the right to choose is paramount to acceptance of a behavior, regardless of which side you are on.*

*I do not see a situation where forcing everyone to accept behaviors of everyone else can be sustainable. Acceptance of the right to choose, not necessarily acceptance of the choice should be the goal. If my son, John, chose to smoke cigarettes, I could coach him on the impacts on health, but eventually I would accept his right to choose even if I did not accept his choice.*

*I am not attempting to equate being gay with smoking, and acceptance to choose not matter what the choice applies to many of life's choices.*

On July 18, 1969, Senator Ted Kennedy was driving a car away from a party he attended on a small Massachusetts island called Chappaquiddick. He was joined by one of the partygoers, Mary Jo Kopechne.

One account of the drive away from the party was that Kennedy had pulled over onto a private road. It may not have been the road he expected, and he began to back up. He may have been startled by the eyewitness that saw him go down the wrong road, because as he headed in what may have been his intended direction, he began driving more quickly than he should have been on the particular road he was on and possibly then took a wrong turn onto Dike Road. Dike road was not the one that would have taken the two to the ferry and eventually to Ms. Kopechne's hotel.

Apparently, realizing too late that he was on the wrong road and headed for a wooden bridge that he thought may not hold his car, he applied the brakes too late and the car ended up driving off the side of the bridge, landing the car on its roof in the water.

Kennedy managed to get himself out of the car and later recounted the episode to include several attempts to rescue Ms. Kopechne. Based on his testimony, two other men assisted with the attempted rescue to no avail. Rather than letting the other rescuers take him to his hotel across the channel, he swam the five hundred feet across managed to end up in his hotel room.

He told the two men he was with that he would report the incident, but never did and went about the next day as if nothing had happened.

Ultimately, Kennedy pled guilty of leaving the scene of an accident and received a sentence of two months in jail, all of which were suspended

## July 19, 1969

*Teddy, I hope that your account of your accident that led to the death of that poor girl is correct. It is certainly a bad situation for everyone concerned. You need to accept whatever becomes of this and move on. I am afraid that your chances of running a nationwide campaign may be slim with this public incident on your record.*

*It is unfortunate that if you have the last name "Kennedy," bad luck follows you. It seems as if we are either in sunshine or a thunderstorm, constant fodder for the political meteorologist.*

*I believe the bridge described in the news account of your accident is the same one that we used to throw rocks off back when*

*we were young. We would spend hours looking for the best rocks to skip across the channel. The flat ones were good, but if they had the right curves and you threw them right, you could get some very nice skips across the water. Of course it always helped when the water was as still as a sheet of glass.*

*This sounds callous, I am sure no one will read this, but you always had difficulty getting the stones across the channel.*

On July 20, 1969, Apollo 11 landed on the moon. The challenge that President Kennedy set for the country, and more specifically NASA, was half over. The second half was to bring them home safely, which of course was achieved. The next day, Neil Armstrong became the first person to walk on the surface of the moon. He was soon joined by Buzz Aldrin, as they became the first to explore the Earth's nearest celestial body.

Four days later, the experiments and rock collecting was complete. The astronauts left the surface of the moon, headed back to Earth and splashed down in the Pacific Ocean within minutes of the recovery ship.

Since no one knew what radiation or possible bacteria, viruses or other pathogens that may be on the moon, the astronauts were treated as though they were radioactive and were confined to a quarantine capsule for three weeks until it was determined that they were safe to interact with others.

## July 20, 1969

*I watched television today as Neil Armstrong stepped onto the surface of the moon. It was a very proud moment for me as it showed the capability of this country to do extraordinary things.*

*I must give credit where credit is due.*

*Jackie and I went for a stroll in the back yard of the White House one day. It was an especially clear night and warm. The lights from DC were not drowning out the stars from putting on a big show. They were sprinkled all over the sky, including the moon shining brightly on the horizon. We were talking about leadership and how serving the country in my capacity relied on me to not only lead the various departments at a high level, but also, similarly, lead the country.*

*Just like the leader of a large company needs to stretch his employers to do the best that they can with a goal of beating the competition, the President should also look for ways to inspire the country to do the best they can.*

*We were discussing ideas on how I could inspire the country to demonstrate that we have the best system in the world - something that does not necessarily require saber rattling.*

*All of a sudden, Jackie pointed to the sky and said, "That's it." I said, "What's it? Reaching to the stars?" She said, "No, reaching to the moon. The United States should be the first country to step foot on the moon."*

*Brilliant!*

*When I challenged the country to put a man on the moon and bring him home by the end of the decade, I did not really know what it would take, but I did not really think it would be possible in such a short timeframe. I was told by some of the scientists that, in theory, it was possible, but there is a long way from theory to execution. It was just a few years ago when we started shooting rockets into the air and got them to not fall back uncontrolled.*

*This achievement of walking on the moon should be a message for generations to come that when this country puts its mind, energy, resources and ingenuity toward something we will achieve our goal. The uniqueness of how this country was founded gives Americans a breadth of opportunity to achieve that is unmatched by any other country in the history of civilization.*

*Neil Armstrong's quote of "One small step for Man, one giant leap for mankind" was brilliant. I hope he was paying attention to the controls on the approach to the moon's surface and not thinking that quip up. I am certain there were no cue cards waiting for him on the moon.*

*It is good that we are often reminded of what we can achieve if we work together. Even though I only participated in World War II, I was amazed by the accomplishments the United States was able to achieve. Transforming a company from one that makes playing cards, to one that makes parachutes is an example how everyone pulled together for a common goal. I hope that we never find ourselves in a position where we are not able to recognize a common goal, and then do what is necessary to achieve it.*

*I am amazed by the scientific achievements that it took to land a piece of equipment, loaded with an important cargo of astronauts, and return them back to Earth, safely! All with equipment that was made in the USA. I know many people with many skills were involved in this achievement and my hat is off to each one of them. They should all be proud of the accomplishment of the entire team. If you think about it, it is also amazing that schoolchildren around the country, and world, could see the landing happen AS it was happening on television. The history books are now written real-time as they unfold.*

Max Yasgur became an instant celebrity when he provided the use of his farm for what became not only a standard for outdoor music festivals, but provided a backdrop for the introduction of many relatively new rock and roll musical groups. The Woodstock Music and Art Fair was held for three days beginning August 15, 1969.

Even the periodic rain could not diminish the enthusiasm of the nearly half a million crowd. For all the top performers that were at Woodstock, notable rock and roll legends were noticeably absent. The Beatles, The Doors, Joni Mitchell, Jethro Tull, Frank Zappa, The Byrds, and Bob Dylan were among the top of the chart groups/performers that for one reason or another did not attend. Some did not recognize the potential significance of the event and some had prior engagements. Some say that John Lennon turned down the invitation to the Beatles because they would not put Yoko Ono on the agenda.

Rain delays pushed the three-day event into a fourth day. Festivals goers that stayed for the final act were treated early on Monday with a two-hour concert by Jimi Hendrix, whose rendition of the Star Spangled Banner is still attempted to be replicated by budding guitar players.

## August 19, 1969

*Woodstock started out as another music festival, but judging by the reports from that New York farm, it may have been the best one ever. I did not see that the Beatles made it, but many popular music groups attended. My father said that you relate most to the music when you were thirteen. That must be why it is difficult for me to relate to today's music. There is a big difference between the ballroom dancing that I am used to and the dancing that goes on with today's music. Do men and women touch each other when they dance anymore?*

*I have seen some of the groups that were listed as performing at the Woodstock music festival on Ed Sullivan. I am not certain how Mr. Sullivan has gotten to a point where he follows these young musicians, but they seem to engender excitement in his television show, so that cannot be all bad. As long as the advertisers keep providing funding, I do not see where he will change directions.*

*Between the newspaper, and his show I seem to get an interesting perspective of the world. Of course, the nightly news helps fill in the blanks.*

On November 18, 1969, the ambassador to the United Kingdom from 1938 to 1940 and patriarch of the Kennedy family died.

Joe Kennedy's eighty-one years were full of many experiences that left a mark on the political fabric of the United States including being father to a president and two senators.

Joe was a Harvard graduate and made the majority of his wealth as an investor in the stock market, gaining experience from his days as a banker after he graduated from college. Joe's investments in the 1920s resulted in a quick amassment of a good-sized fortune for that era. Joe cash out of the market just before the stock market crash leading to the Great Depression. He took he cash and began investing in real estate and managed to get an almost 5000% return on his real estate investments in six years. Some say he was more than lucky.

## November 19, 1969

*You had a long run Dad. I am sorry that I did not finish my term. I know how disappointed you must have been when something did not get finished.*

On December 15, 1969, President Nixon announced the withdrawal of 50,000 United States troops from Vietnam within the following four months.

Within the next two years, troops continued to be brought home to a level of about 70,000 coming home by the beginning of 1972. The North Vietnamese saw the weakness in the posture of the United States as an opportunity to attempt to increase their push into the south. The United States and South Vietnamese forces managed to repel the invasion, but it led to a ceasefire early in 1973.

The United States eventually pulled out. It did not take long for North Vietnamese to make a final and successful push into South Vietnamese territory.

## December 16, 1969

*Dick's withdrawal of troops from Vietnam perhaps signals the light at the end of the tunnel for the War. It has been more than unpopular; it has been a drain on the resources of the United States. Our ability to fight a war where neither side is particular fond of our involvement likely does not make sense. I hope that we learn from this and our approach to involvement in regional skirmishes will change in the future.*

*The challenge that we have in being involved in regional differences is trying to choose which side to support. We could choose what we think is correctly one year, and something changes like new elections or their leadership turns out to be opposite of what we think should lead their country to the most democratic system.*

*The other challenge is picking the right side in the first place. It is very difficult to determine the difference between what leaders say their position is about foreign and domestic matters and what they actually do when they are in a leadership position or have our support. A leader may promise change, but not be specific on what that change is, or what it may mean to their country. In a matter of months or years, the 'change' may not only not be in the best interest of the country and the citizens may not feel they got the results for which they voted. If citizens are duped, how do we know we are not going to find ourselves in the same position?*

*Perhaps what we should focus on is assisting in the foundation of a country that can survive no matter what person happens to be the leader. The balance of powers that exists in the United States is our foundation for that possible outcome. One person should not be in a position to make unilateral decisions because they are what he/she thinks is best. The establishment of laws and ensuring that the laws are followed, all tied with control of funding are important divisions of power that should not be circumvented or ignored.*

# Chapter 11 – 1970

The National Environmental Policy Act (NEPA) allowed the creation of the President's Council on Environmental Quality. Some say that this bill was triggered in part by an oil spill in California. The bill took almost a year from introduction to Presidential signature, which finally was accomplished on New Year's Day in 1970.

The NEPA is broad in scope as it can be applied to virtually anything the federal government decides to do. As part of the normal thumbs up or down determination on new government projects or activities, the Act decrees that the environment should be one of the factors to be included in that decision.

The lack of specifics concerning the scope, degree and methodology to determine the degree of environmental impact makes it difficult to perform the environmental assessment. This vagueness also makes difficult to create policies that will not blow with the political breeze of who happens to be in charge. Emptying a lake of its water in northern California so the people in southern California can wash their private jets may escape NEPA application of policies, while the creation of desalination plants along the southern California may be halted for its impact on the coast.

The person or group responsible for clearing NEPA policies is responsible for completing an Environmental Impact Statement (EIS). In the EIS, the author is to provide a written description in five major areas.

1) **The environmental impacts of the action.** For example, "Draining the lake will result in fish flopping around in a bed of mud until they die."

2) **Any adverse environmental impacts that cannot be avoided.** In this scenario and example may be, "The dead fish will smell bad."

3) **Reasonable alternatives to the proposed solution.** The author of the EIS may expand upon, "Fly the planes to northern California to wash them."

4) **Relationship between short-term uses of the environment and enhancement of long-term productivity.** For example, "Washing the planes in southern California would keep the pilots local in case the owner of the jet needed to go somewhere."

5) **Any irreversible and irretrievable commitments of resources.** "Pray for rain."

## January 2, 1970

*I have always thought that we should give back to our environment what we take out. Stewardship of the environment in which we live is critical if we wish to leave a better place for our offspring than what was left for us.*

*Stewardship may be one of the most important goals that we could achieve, particularly as it relates to impact on future generations. The day we live for today and delay taking action, saving problems for tomorrow, is the day we no longer are thinking of our children and grandchildren.*

*Rachel Carson's book brought this home to me as I was thinking about things I can do for the future. Our country has some of the best scientists in the world. We should be able to research chemicals before we use them, particularly if they have the ability to contaminate our food supply or leach into our water supply.*

*The National Environmental Policy Act is an excellent step towards making certain due diligent research should be conducted prior to embarking on new projects that may jeopardize the environment.*

*We must resist allowing commercial entities, such as chemical companies, to overpower the discussion. They have a right to produce a product and receive a fair profit. However, if the balance of impact on our duties to be stewards is weighted higher that the companies right to profit, then our stewardship duties must prevail. Incremental costs of finding new solutions that do not adversely affect the environment should be the rule not the exception.*

*On the obverse, a flattened frog in the middle of a highway should not be an excuse to require walking.*

Gaylord Nelson, Senator from Wisconsin is often referred to as the father of Earth Day. As with the National Environmental Policy Act the California oil spill made an impact on people that we may not be taking care of the Earth as well as we should. Almost a hundred staff was hired to promote the idea of environmental awareness, and a new government industry was born.

The first Earth Day was held on April 22nd and gained popularity quickly, particularly with educational institutions as thousands of schools participated in the first Earth Day and each one since.

# April 22, 1970

*Earth Day is a great concept and technique to encourage focus on what we can do to give back to the Earth. We cut down trees to build our houses, it is appropriate that we plant trees to replace what we took. While the single day dedicated to a refocus on the Earth and nature is an admirable activity, I would suggest that paying attention to how we interact with the Earth should be a practice, not a one-day event.*

*Wasting our resources and not paying attention to impacts of what we do as it relates to the Earth's resources should be behaviors that we continue to eliminate. If Earth Day can encourage that change in behaviors without Governmental regulations and legislation, then the spirit of Earth Day will have succeeded. For if we need to rely on Government to set the conservation goals for Americans, then the bar becomes a political level and rather than behavior change from within, it can be perceived as behavior change from oppression.*

*Although there were obviously extenuating circumstances, when I gave the challenge to go to the moon, hopefully, part of the motivation was the leadership that I was attempting to portray. Similar leadership focused on how we treat the resources of the Earth can be much more powerful than oppressive legislation that could turn into a political issue and detract from the true intention of the goal.*

On May 4th, the National Guard killed four Kent State students and wounded nine in a spray of bullets that lasted less than fifteen seconds. Shootings occurred during anti-war, student protests that grew violent, resulting in the deaths of four demonstrators by the Ohio National Guard. The conflict was between seventy-seven National Guard volunteers versus a couple thousand students.

President Nixon, who had campaigned on his intentions to end the Vietnam War, ordered a "Cambodian Incursion" to begin, committing troops to a new front. This direction was announced on April 30th. Students at Kent State began protesting on the next day, May 1st. A generally peaceful protest began getting bigger and more violent. Public destruction was happening all around the area surround the campus.

By May 4th, the violence and participation escalated despite school administration's attempts to keep violence at bay. The National Guard was called in to disperse the crown. The presence of armed and uniformed guardsmen spurred the crowd to begin rock throwing.

The guardsmen attempted to use tear gas, which was ineffective because of winds and the protestors simply threw the canisters back at the guardsmen. It is unclear what started the bullets flying, but was over quick – resulting in four dead students, one dying almost immediately and one who was paralyzed.

## May 5, 1970

*Tragedy in Ohio. It is likely that not all information has been discovered or reported on what happened at Kent State, but the fact that four students are now not going to walk down the aisle to receive their diploma is tragic.*

*Riots like these can be prevented. Most people that protest do not do so with the intention of becoming violent. The Ohio Guardsmen may have overreacted in their approach to the situation, leading to a rise in emotions and an eventual backlash that was not controlled.*

*Whether it is emotions on the side of the rioter, or emotions on the side of the riot preventer both sides have the potential to be overcome by those emotions and exceed their training or understanding of what is right.*

*The challenge is that it is a bit of a catch twenty-two. You want to protect innocent people and avoid any escalation. Your mere presence, however, is sometimes enough to incite behaviors that would otherwise be controlled.*

> *Hindsight and foresight may be twenty/twenty, but fine lines become blurred when the time is now.*

National Environmental Policy Act, Earth Day, and the Environment Protection Agency – a triumvirate of environmental events on President Nixon's watch. The third leg of the stool of President Nixon's environmental focus during 1970, in the middle of his first term, was the establishment of the Environmental Protection Agency on December 2nd.

The EPA began as a brainchild of the President and was initially started with the stroke of the executive order pen and later given approval by House and Senate hearings. The President's goal was to consolidate a number of environmentally focused governmental groups into a single administrative body with teeth of enforcement and fines.

Given President Nixon's vision in creating this agency, it is curious why the federal building that houses the EPA got a name change in 2013 to the "William Jefferson Clinton Federal Building."

## December 3, 1970

> *Nice job, Dick. We may need to make you an honorary Democrat. Of course, establishing an agency like this makes a lot of sense. There are many facets of the environment that needed an umbrella organization that can pay attention to the environment as a whole.*

On December 29, 1970, President Nixon signed the Occupational Safety and Health Act into law. The act had two major parts, a focus on safety and health in work environments and establishment of a method for reporting of safety and health issues through whistleblowing.

Four months after the law went into effect, the agency to carry out the law was established – the Occupational Safety and Health Administration.

There is a constant debate over the effectiveness of this governmental bureaucracy. Some contend that the cost of enforcement of the regulations outweighs the very small amount of convictions (twelve in thirty years) due to lack of adherence to the regulations. Others take the position that without the regulations and threat of prosecution that employers would not pay attention to the health and safety of their workforce.

## December 30, 1970

*As America transformed from a primarily farming industry, where the goal was to make certain that everyone had enough to eat to an industrial economy, workers transformed from working for themselves in a self-imposed work environment to an environment that was primarily directed by the company with which they worked.*

*This shift allowed for an opportunity for companies to take advantage of their power as wage providers. Workers were encouraged to live close to the company, even in housing provided by the company. In many cases, this put the health and welfare of workers in the hands of these industrial companies. Company housing, company stores, and company towns were springing up around the large smokestacks of American progress.*

*The challenge was that companies began taking advantage of this situation as profits became harder to obtain and, unfortunately, came at the backs of the workers. There were few government regulations to put these negative consequences on the workers in check. So, government regulations were needed to protect the workers.*

*The Occupational Safety and Health Act is another piece of legislation that falls in the category of forcing employers to provide an environment that is safe and pays attention to the welfare of people working for that company. I believe that forcing companies to be focused on employee welfare should not always be punitive. Governments have the option to provide rewards for safe environments rather than only fines. For example, tax rebates also directly affect an organization's bottom line, as much as fines that can be a negative impact. In the larger picture, the bureaucratic organization that assesses fines and conducts inspections may be able to be reduced as it focuses on positive reinforcement.*

# Chapter 12 – The Liberal Dilemma

## February 2, 1971

*The more I pay attention to politics from the outside, the more intrigued I am by the inconsistencies and incongruences that are taken on by each party – more than just the fact that Dick took office last year.*

*For example, some Liberals tend to favor the ability for women to decide whether their unborn child should live or be aborted. Some Conservatives believe that women should not have that ability to make that decision. On one hand, it is a right to choose; on the other hand, it is a choice to end a life. As the choice argument is honed, it moves more to a question of the woman being able to be in control of her body and if you do not agree, you are against the woman's right to decide what to do with her body.*

*There, then, is introduced a continuum from conception to birth as to when is it tolerable for the women to exercise her decision to end her pregnancy. The argument extends to a discussion about whether 'life' starts at conception or at birth. A majority of people may be in favor of a woman's right to decide to end her pregnancy if it is considered okay as long as the baby is not viable. In other words, if the baby could not otherwise live outside the womb, then it is tolerable for the decision to be to terminate the pregnancy.*

*Then, the question is when is the baby viable? As technology changes, it becomes more feasible for life to exist earlier in the pregnancy. So, why should viability be a consideration? If the fetus is considered a life at thirty-five weeks one year and thirty years later is considered a life based on viability at twenty-five weeks, it is not life that is changing; it is the technology of the medical profession that is dictating the timing.*

*Therefore, a woman can choose to terminate her pregnancy as long as the medical profession can make it viable. What happens if members of the medical profession are able to take a newly conceived egg out of the uterus and are able to get it to grow 'viably' in an artificial womb environment. It may seem not possible today, but could be feasible at some point.*

*Therefore, at what point should the woman own the decision whether or not to end the pregnancy? Viability is arbitrary and based on technology of the medical profession.*

*If the argument was straightforward, then there may not be so much effort put in to changing the language or context for making the argument.*

*Rather than communicating the issue as one that deals with a woman's decision of whether to end her pregnancy, it becomes a woman's right to choose what to do with her body. Even though, it can be argued that it is not her body, but a life that her body is sustaining. If the sustenance can be continued without need for her body, is termination killing? Moreover, should the woman have a right to kill?*

*The Liberal Dilemma*

*Pregnancy termination is a very public example of the liberal dilemma. As I see the two major political parties be continually wedged apart, I am discouraged. Discouraged by the challenge that I see each party has ahead. The focus of both parties is getting more greatly honed in on achieving votes rather than communicating convictions – convictions driven by the Constitution and laws. The focus is moving away from creating and maintaining an environment where all Americans have an opportunity to choose their destiny. Sometimes I do not know whether I align more to the Democrats or Republicans – or a version of both.*

*Trying to make everyone happy often seems to create a series of bipolar situations, wedge issues, that I am calling "The Liberal Dilemma".*

*The Liberal Dilemma is based on the inclusiveness challenge that continuously becomes more systemically embraced by the Democratic Party. This of course is not unique to the Democrat Party. As is the general nature and goal of the political process today, both political parties are focused on including as many people as possible. To win elections and ensure representation of the views of your party, every vote is important. The challenge is the wedge issues that create divisiveness, which is the dilemma. If you drive enough wedges in a stump, you end up with many splinters. This situation, of course, is not unique to politics.*

*Getting as many people together that share your views starts in the preschool sandbox and on the grade school playground. After a long morning of reading, writing, and ciphering, the young, impressionable minds are ready for a break. Recess. After an initial short period of observable chaos, the children decide they are ready to be organized. It is the youngster with the strongest personality (and often, loudest voice) that gets to decide what playground game everyone plays at recess. I tended to choose football. This behavior seems to be a natural occurrence. It continues through school and into the workforce.*

*I do not know a lot about birds, but when they fly in a wedge formation, it appears that there is one bird that is in charge. It appears that the bird that is in front is the leader. Unless, of course, birds are OK with being led from behind. There is something that the lead bird has that causes the others to follow in formation.*

*A good example of moving opinions to your side happens in business almost every time the sales department meets with the product or service delivery department. Sales has opinion s of what they can sell, Product Delivery has opinions of what they can make. When they get together to determine the product or service focus for plan for the next five years, they often cannot agree to direction. The group that gets to the CEO first, and convinces him/her their side, will normally prevail.*

*The challenge that manifests is that when the broad net is cast to gather as many people to follow you, that you catch a broad range of passionate people, not all passionate in the same thing. Moreover, the challenge becomes a dilemma when the passions do not always play together well in the sandbox.*

*The Liberal Dilemma is a quandary of multiple passions playing in the same sandbox, following the lead bird.*

*Not getting too far away from the playground, another analogy comes to mind. A child's game that helps them make decisions - Rock, Paper, Scissors. The premise is that first, there is a decision that needs to be made. For example, assume that the decision is whether to play tetherball or jump rope. Two children face off with their hands poised to determine who gets to choose. Obviously, neither child is the loudmouth leader of the playground that insists on football.*

*The winner of the faceoff gets to make the decision. With one hand held out flat with the palm facing upward, the other hand strikes in open-faced hand three times with the striking hand in a fist. On the third strike, a choice is made and exposed verbally, simultaneously with both of the opposing decision makers. Exposing a rock is when the striking hand stays clenched in a fist. Exposing paper is when the striking hand is stretched flat and strikes the open-faced hand like a sideways clap. Exposing scissors, is when the striking hand strikes the open-faced hand similar to the rock, but with the forefinger and middle finger stretched out like a peace sign.*

*As it goes, Rock beats Scissors because the Rock smashes the Scissors. Scissors beats Paper, because the Scissors cut the Paper. Paper beats Rock, because Paper wraps up the Rock.*

*Not one of Rock, Paper, or Scissors is better than the other. All of them can become overcome by another one.*

*To match the triumvirate of the child's decision tool, Liberalism (which can be expanded to mean societies social issues) can be simplified into three competing domains: Social, Ecological, and Economic.*

- *Social Liberalism incudes policies designed to provide social assistance. Examples include voting rights, equal opportunity (civil rights), and immigration.*
- *Ecological Liberalism includes ecological programs that are designed to protect the environment.*
- *Economic Liberalism includes economic programs and business relationship such as taxes, housing and trade.*

*Rock – is tied to Social Liberalism. The Rock symbolizes the foundation, just as social aspects are typically described of as the foundation of society.*

*Paper – is tied to Ecological Liberalism. The Paper Salvage that the British introduced during the War was an example of recycling programs that all countries developed.*

*Scissors – is tied to Economic Liberalism. Scissors represent cutting, or not cutting budgets.*

*Rock, Paper, Scissors is a relatively simple construct, but may help explain and prepare for oppositional views on the difficult issues that the Country faces. It is a construct that may help policy setting that is able to seek out balances among each of the three dimensions, ultimately being even more inclusive.*

A modern example of the application of the Rock, Paper, and Scissors concept is in the area of energy. It is clear that the blood in the arteries of the economy is the energy needed to run cars, heat houses, illuminate classroom, and keep the internet operational. It is also clear that alternative sources of energy need to be developed to sustain the growth in need for energy – oil and coal are not good for the environment. The dilemma is in determining in what sources to invest.

Wind power is one potential area. Electricity is generated by the natural flow of wind turning a turbine and generating electricity. "Paper" would say that using nature to turn the turbines is much better than burning fossil fuels. "Scissors" would say that the cost of producing the turbines for wind power does not justify the electricity that is generated. There are also a couple of internal conflicts within "Paper" – the number of birds that are killed by each turbine and the destruction of the aesthetics of the countryside with wind farms.

A similar potential method for generating power is to harness sunlight with solar power. Similar to wind, "Paper" debaters would argue that solar energy is much cleaner than the fossil fuels. "Scissors" debaters have issues with the current costs versus the benefits while other "Paper" people have an issue with the birds that are fried by the heat of the glass panels used to collect the sun's energy and the negative impact of aesthetics of vast expanses of solar panels. Airplane pilots, too, are concerned with being blinded by the mirror effect of the panels.

Another example of the application of the Rock, Paper, and Scissors concept is a basic one – the expansion of social programs (Rock) versus the money to pay for them (Scissors). Expanding social programs without a sound economical way to pay for them is fiscally irresponsible. Not providing temporary, safety net services when you can afford to provide them is socially irresponsible.

The other "Rock" area that tends to be contentious is whether the collective people (government) should pay for choices.

Should the freedoms of one segment of the population to make one choice over another one be infringed upon by being forced to pay for the choices of another?  Examples of this include; birth control, abortion, and religion.

# Chapter 13 – 1971

The Public Health Cigarette Smoking Act was signed into law on April 1, 1971 and essentially meant the end of Joe Camel. In addition to mandating a warning on packages of cigarettes ("Warning: The Surgeon General Has Determined that Cigarette Smoking is Dangerous to Your Health"), about nine months after the law being in effect, a ban on cigarette advertisement on television was in effect. Interesting, for a while into the ban, cigarette commercials were still allowed during New Year's Day broadcasts of college football games. Perhaps they needed time to transition to alcohol commercials to pay for the bowl games.

The FCC's argument to banning the cigarette commercials stemmed from their interpretation of the Fairness Doctrine. They maintained that since there was not a feasible opportunity for opponents of cigarette smoking to air commercials that described how cigarette smoking is bad for you, commercials selling cigarettes should not be allowed.

# April 2, 1971

*I understand that cigarette smoking is a choice and that the focus should be on education of the negative health impacts of smoking. My biggest concern with the Cigarette Smoking Act is that government is using the power of the purse to attempt to change behaviors. I am not certain of the overall fairness of the ability of government to tax the people, use the money to fund areas that are a stretch as to their necessity to be funded at the federal level, and then use the fact that there is federal funding to control those areas.*

*The fact that government funds and regulates television gives either the legislative or executive branches the ability to tell television what to do, what shows to broadcast, and possibly at some point, what to say. We have gone to war to prevent other governments to control their people I arguably similar ways. I understand that I am stretching the point, but it is a direction that I see America possibly heading unless government power through the purse is reduced. The breadth of the influence of that control could be limitless unless somehow held in check. I am hopeful that the system of checks and balances and the ability of the people to put people in office that will not let that happen will prevail.*

*Franklin Roosevelt made big strides at a time when big strides were desperately needed. However, even he became to be seen by many to begin to have too tight of a grasp on how government was run, particularly when he was into his fourth term in office. Roosevelt's grip on the office of the President was only released when he died in office on April 12, 1945. Ultimately, an Amendment to the Constitution was adopted that limits Presidential terms to two.*

*As long as the balance of powers at the federal level exists and people are truly enabled to select electorates that can put the expansion of powers in check, the balance of powers may not be an issue. However, if the balance of powers gets misaligned and/or the people are no longer strongly participatory in the process, we may have challenges ahead and it may take a situation like the four terms of King Teddy to waken the people.*

On June 17, 1971, President Nixon addressed the nation from the White House briefing room with one of his most memorable speeches – the initiation of his War Against Drugs. It is somewhat ironic that he called this offensive against drug abuse a war. The same population that was protesting the war in Vietnam was the target audience of this new war.

With this speech to the American people, Nixon described his address to Congress where he pushed for the compilation of a number of drug-related federal programs into a single initiative – similar to other Presidential initiatives like the War on Poverty and the War on Terrorism. A move that makes some sense as it has the potential to eliminate some waste in program overlap and focus funding in a coordinated way.

President Nixon also noted the appointment of D. Jerome Jaffe as Special Consultant to the President for Narcotics and Dangerous Drugs. Nixon was aware that the expansion of government was not a trademark of his party and stated that he was reluctant to expand the executive branch – "I very much hesitate always to bring some new responsibility into the White House, because there are so many here, and I believe in delegating those responsibilities to the departments. But I consider this problem so urgent – I also found that it was scattered so much throughout the Government, with so much conflict, without coordination – that it had to be brought into the White House."

## June 18, 1971

*I see that Dick appointed someone to focus on the illegal drug challenges that face the nation. Even though the perception of Dick is that he is adding to government, and that in his opinion is not a good thing, I think it is inevitable.*

*Some may say that this is a move that will alienate young voters, and it may, but it is a focus that is important. I am interested to see how they approach the issue. Will they target directly to the youth with an education program? Alternatively, will they target the sources and distributors of the drugs? Or both.*

*I know if I was a young man and the federal government tried to tell me how I should manage my body, I would likely revolt, unless my mother was President. My reaction would probably be "Do you think I'm stupid? I can handle myself enough to know when too much is too much and limit or eliminate my use." In fact, I remember when I was the age of the target audience and if you did not want me to do something, the worst thing to do was to tell me not to do it. Instant focus on the prohibited behavior. "Why are you telling me what to do? Why do you think I cannot control myself? Why is it such a big deal?"*

*Of course, now that I am older, I understand better some of the reasons why it may be better not to even start drug use. A bit of a catch twenty-two.*

The twenty-sixth Amendment to the United States Constitution was adopted on July 1, 1971. This amendment lowered the voting age from twenty-one to eighteen.

In 1954, President Eisenhower introduced the notion of giving eighteen year olds the right to vote. An excerpt from his address – "For years our citizens between the ages of eighteen and twenty-one have, in time of peril, been summoned to fight for America. They should participate in the political process that produces this fateful summons. I urge Congress to propose to the States a constitutional amendment permitting citizens to vote when they reach the age of eighteen."

In 1970, Eisenhower's words were heeded as President Nixon signed an executive order tied to the Voting Rights Act of 1965. However, he did not fully legislate from the oval office, he engaged the Attorney General to expedite a court ruling on the constitutionality of his amendment to that Act with his executive pen. Oregon and Texas quickly challenged Nixon's executive order, necessitating a ruling by the Supreme Court. The Supreme Court overruled Nixon's pen and declared the reduction of the voting age to eighteen valid for Federal elections, but unconstitutional for State and local elections because, according to the Constitution, the States are responsible for election laws for their State.

This put the rules pertaining to eighteen to twenty year olds in a bit of chaos. While eighteen year olds could vote on Federal ballots, it would be up to each State to determine its laws regarding voting age for State and local elections. Some decreased the age, some left it at twenty-one.

Consider what the operations looked like at an individual precinct in a State that did not lower the voting age. Rather than having a single ballot that included all federal, state, and local issues and candidates, there needed to be a separate ballot for federal issues and candidates for one set of voters (eighteen and over) and a second ballot for state and local issues for a second set of voters (twenty-one and over). The election officials at each precinct needed to keep everything straight.

An amendment to the Constitution was drafted to fix the problem and align the voting age for all Federal, State, and local elections. On July 1, 1971, which was only a year after Nixon's executive order and just in time before the next general election in 1972, North Carolina became the thirty-eighth State to ratify the Twenty-sixth Amendment to the Constitution allowing the certification of its adoption.

## July 2, 1971

*The argument is compelling that if you are old enough to fight for your country in the military, you should be old enough to vote for or against the people who have the power to draft you into service or direct where you will serve. Access to information is much more pervasive than it has been historically to allow for more informed citizens as they head to the voting booth. Schools are well suited to help young people understand what it means to be a contributing and participating member of society and the value of their one vote.*

*Most of the parents of today's eighteen year olds had direct or indirect involvement with World War II and understand the strong sense of nationalism and purpose that was prevalent at that time. These parents are certain to understand the value of voting rights and the positive message in extending those rights to their young sons and daughters.*

*An interesting potential consequence of the Vietnam War and changing the voting age now is that if the Republicans are seen as the party that dismantled the War, they may get a surge of votes from the newly anointed eighteen, nineteen and twenty-year-old voters. This may be the start of a surge in Republican victories. Related to this, I also have noted that a consequence of the draft is an increase in male teachers as they found a way to avoid the draft without needing to move to Canada. It will be interesting to see how this uptick in participation in education by males will influence the education system. On the other hand, maybe I just have too much time to think.*

Nixon Shock was the term applied to the lifting of gold as the backing for United States currency on August 15, 1970. Nixon needed to find a way to counter the effects of the high amounts of Federal spending that had happened in the recent history and one way to counter those effects is to relieve the pressure of the gold standard.

There were two pressures that forced such a dramatic announcement, the rest of the world gaining economic strength and high spending by the United States. Other countries were gaining economic output, lowering the overall percentage of the strength of the United States. As other countries were strengthening, the United States was economically shooting itself in the foot by spending a lot of money on the Vietnam War and Great Society social programs that drew down resources over the prior decade.

In the decade of the sixties, gold stock was cut in half and therefore the backing of United States currency suffered. Nixon put the brakes on the economic bleeding, likely preventing a run on the banks that could have caused a Depression similar to four decades earlier. He issued an executive order that removed gold as a need for backing of the United States dollar, put a ninety-day ceiling on wages and prices, and imposed a ten percent tax on imports. The freeze on inflation and encouragement of domestic production were attempts to temper the impact of the "shock" of dropping the gold standard.

Part of Nixon's address to the nation (and the world) was to explain that if Americans travel or buy foreign products, it might cost a little more. He went on to explain that if Americans buy products made in America while in America, the American dollar would "be worth just as much tomorrow as it is today."

Many say that while the economic move that Nixon made was good in the short-term, that it lead to economic doldrums for another decade as the world was rebalancing to the lack of the gold standard. The uncertainty and equilibrium disturbance that follows economic shifts is often difficult for monetary traders to endure effectively.

## August 16, 1971

*One of the important roles of the United States is to provide stability to the rest of the world. This stability is primarily in economic and political terms. Of course, to the extent that the world is economically stable, the need for political or military-enhanced stability is lessened.*

*When there is limited economic stability in a given section of the world or even a particular country, that region or country tends to be more inclined to lash out in some manner – politically, militarily, or some other way. In fact, maintaining a high level of economic stability may lead to the ability of the United States to pull back somewhat on military spending which often acts as the stick for geopolitical stability. Economic instability likely requires an uptick in military spending to help get the pendulum to neutral.*

*Dick's announcement that the United States currency will be no longer tied to gold may be shortsighted. The removal of the tie to gold may fulfill a bit of the current slide in economic prosperity, but it will have a negative effect on world currencies, allowing them to be more volatile. This volatility can lead to uncertainty, which can affect geopolitical stability.*

*It also is a move that will likely not be able to be reversed. Once the basis for the United States Dollar is removed, it will be very difficult to go back to gold as the standard for the value of our currency. In addition, the opportunity for abuse of this lack of stable backing is raised. To maintain global stability, it will be necessary for controls to be in place that do not allow the Congress or the President to control the money supply in any way that is not consistent with the norm.*

# Chapter 14 – 1972

From February 21 through February 28, 1972, President Nixon paid a visit to China. Nixon became the first sitting President to visit the People's Republic of China and made great strides in opening nation-to-nation relations.

Many saw this visit as a bold move for the President. While there were behind-the-scenes meetings to set the stage for this historic event, it surprised many back in the United States even though Nixon had been suggesting that a meeting with China was of strategic importance to the United States.

Even though this was an initial meeting, Nixon and the Chinese had many areas to discuss. His initial meeting was with Chairman Mao and the remainder of his week in China was in discussions with Chinese Premier Zhou Enlai. Some of these areas included; the Vietnam War and how to reduce Soviet involvement, future political relationships, and trade with Taiwan.

Back in the United States, Nixon's trip was hailed as a big success and was one of his biggest achievements of his Presidency.

## February 24, 1972

*I knew Henry Kissinger was an excellent pick. I am certain that he had a larger hand in Dick's trip to China than has been reported. It is a good direction for the United States to be focusing on the global economy, and including China in our economic and political policies makes a lot of sense. China could be the new bastion of stability to the world's future. Open trade between the Chinese and the United States has a lot of promise economically and for stability in Asia. We need to make certain that another war like the one three short decades ago never happens again.*

The first of what would be two sets of Strategic Arms Limitation Talks (SALT) were held from 1969 until 1972. Their focus was on freezing the number of strategic ballistic missile launchers between the Soviet Union and the United States. The SALT I Treaty was finally signed at the Moscow Summit by President Nixon and Russian Leonid Brezhnev on May 26, 1972.

## May 27, 1972

*The Strategic Arms Limitation Talks are finally more than talk as there is an agreement that both sided may be able to live with. As with any high level talks such as these, I am certain that both sides will be going back to their citizens and describing how they won for their country. The bottom line is that these discussions completing with an agreement on cutting back on nuclear proliferation means that the world may have won.*
*During my term, I increased spending on defense while communicating that my goal was a lean and fit national defense. Lean, in that I did not want to spend money needlessly. My focus was on what we could do to prevent war, not necessarily to participate in it. However, the things that I invested in where what we needed to be the best in the world. It did not make sense*

*to me to spend money on material that was not the best that we
could produce. If our soldiers need to be, then they should be, the
most well-equipped and ready force in the world.*

Title IX was a section from the Education Amendments of
1972 to the Civil rights Act of 1964. Even though it was only a
section of the amendments, it was one of the most well known and
impactful - especially in the college sports world.

President Nixon signed the bill on June 23, 1972. It
consisted of one sentence that ultimately required specific policy
language to help make the sentence able to be implemented. The
language was, "No person in the United States shall, on the basis of
sex, be excluded from participation in, be denied the benefits of, or
be subjected to discrimination under any education program or
activity receiving federal financial assistance."

Some say that this was a classic case of government
overreach because federal funding was used as the lever. If the
funding for education fully comes from the States, then the federal
government cannot control educational systems through bills like
this or Presidential executive orders. However, when the federal
tether is applied to funding being dispersed back to the States from
which it originally came, then a commensurate amount of control
can also be applied. Equality for women is certainly not an issue
that is very arguable, but the result of the way Title IX was
implemented by the Department of Health, Education and Welfare
was to increase Women's athletics at the expense of some Men's
sports.

During Carter's administration, the Department of Health,
Education and Welfare enacted specific rules that interpreted Title
IX to force equality in spending for athletics between men and
women. Women's sports quickly began to flourish with a booster
shot of funding. Since there was no equal women's sport to football
and men's sports began to be cut, there was more budget for
women's sports. An outcome that Title IX had been created to
produce. Some of the areas that were called out in the language

that colleges were to use to test their equality compliance were equipment and supplies, scheduling of games and practice time, funding for travel, tutoring, coaches compensation, locker rooms and practice facilities, trainer support, and dining and housing.

Before Title IX, women's sports were used to practicing on recreational fields with old equipment, travelling to competitions in private vehicles, and trying to cut corners by sleeping at friend's houses. Title IX created the opportunity for new fields to be built, new equipment to be purchased, better travel to competitions – like flying, and staying at quality hotels. All the while, corresponding men's sports such as golf, tennis, swimming, track and soccer lost funding and programs either reduced or cut.

Title IX resulted in the quickest jump in collegiate athletics competitiveness for women in history. The effects were easily seen in worldwide and Olympic competitions since 1980. From the men's sports perspective, since the implementation was focused on equality of athletes that made the team, little attention was paid to the opportunity cost. More male athletes that want to participate in collegiate sports continue to be turned away than female athletes. From an opportunity standpoint, Title IX tilted the pendulum very much toward women, but had excellent results in achieving the goal of quickly gaining equality for women. There may be a point in time when the opportunity issue is addressed by a fine-tuning of the regulations.

## June 24, 1972

*Title IX is a great opportunity for women. It is easy for a college simply to focus on sports that bring in revenue, but providing the opportunity for women to participate in sports with similar scholarships and budgets makes college sports more equitable among the genders. The issue of equality with race was in some respects easier because it came down to skills. Ultimately, the color of a man's skin did not matter when it came to putting the best team on the field. Sports and life are similar - discrimination has no place in either.*

*Women's equality in sports was a bigger challenge. Ultimately, it took the acceptance of women's sports into the 'men's' organization, the NCAA, to put women on the same footing as men. They needed to have similar rules and be governed similarly. They needed to have resources for scholarships, travel, and coaches similar to men.*

*There are likely to be challenges along the way. Colleges have limited budgets to be able to double the number of athletes that are being supported overnight. Administrators will need to be able to be creative in how this law is implemented. An outcome of reducing the opportunity for men may be inevitable, but would be a shame. The federal government may need to back up the law with funding that will help colleges attain equity quickly without eliminating men's sports and opportunities.*

*A certain impact of an increased level of support for women's sports is stronger performances at the Olympics. One of the best ways to see if the additional focus on women athletes is to be able to see an uptick in performance of women from the United States versus the other countries. I will be interested to follow records and medal counts to see if my supposition is correct.*

Furman v. Georgia was a case that came before the Supreme Court regarding the nationwide consistent application of the death penalty. There were three similar cases before the Supreme Court, each having differing applications of the capital punishment. In one case, the defendant described an accidental killing when his firearm accidentally fired during a robbery. Another case was a rape that occurred during an armed robbery during a home invasion. A third case was one in California that ultimately was not heard by the Supreme Court because the laws in California at the time had no provisions for the application of the death penalty across the board.

The Supreme Court ultimately ruled that application of the death penalty for cases that did not result in a homicide violated the federal protection against cruel and unusual punishment. Special cases would not be applicable.

This ruling resulted in States that had the death penalty as an option to relook at their application of it. They needed to ensure they were not administering the sentence for cases that were non-homicides or somehow discriminatory against the accused.

## June 30, 1972

*The death penalty is a difficult social issue. It is a very long held penalty for serious crimes against fellow man. It does not need to be said that throughout time, the death penalty has been used as the ultimate penalty.*

*Aside from the Supreme Court ruling, one of the challenges that States have in carrying out this punishment is a determination as to whether it is a penalty that is a deterrent for others who may perpetrate a similar crime. Another challenge for consideration is whether the death penalty provides any conclusion to the family of victims of the crime.*

*Currently, the timeframe from the crime to the punishment is likely too long to be much of a deterrent. More criminals have died in appeals or waiting for the death penalty than those that have actually been put to death under the sentence. This does not give potential perpetrators much cause to pause and think about the likelihood for being put to death prior to committing their crime. And. of course, many of them may be in a frame of mind that no punishment weighed in on their decision to commit the crime.*

*The timeframe to carry out the death penalty also may be more of a burden to the family members of the victim than any resolution that may happen because of carrying it out. For many, each appeal is a handful of salt placed in the emotional wound of the original crime. Any details that are resurrected that may have been forgotten can be just as devastating as when they originally happened, extending the pain to the family of the victim.*

*Perhaps, there is an alternative way to punish someone who otherwise would be assessed with the death penalty. The ultimate goal is to erase the convicted criminal from society. The death penalty obvious accomplishes that goal, but maybe there is another alternative.*

*For example, one of the first things that could be done with the convicted person is to shun them from society - create an environment where they will never be heard from, unless the conviction is under appeal. Shutting them out from any interaction with society will eliminate messages from the convict to the outside world. If the victim's families know that the convict will have limited interaction with people and no contact with the outside word, they may be able to get some feeling of closure. Another positive consequence could be that fewer 'shunned' individuals would go down the appellate path since they do not face execution. Just a thought.*

On November 7, 1972, President Nixon was reelected to a second term by an Electoral College landslide. George McGovern managed to carry Massachusetts and the District of Columbia, with Nixon garnering all the remaining votes except one Electoral College vote for Hospers in Virginia. The faithless elector from Virginia was Roger McBride who voted for Libertarian candidate John Hospers. Notably, Hospers' running mate was Theodora Nathan, which became the first electoral vote for a woman in history. Also notable was the fact the McBride became the Libertarian candidate for President in the following, 1976 election.

McGovern's run up to the election was hampered by embarrassment stemming from a bit of a scandal that befell his running mate, Thomas Eagleton. Senator McGovern asked a half dozen Democrats to be on his ticket, all who refused. Finally, the name of Senator Eagleton was given to him and McGovern made Eagleton his choice. Unfortunately, for Senator McGovern, vetting of Senator Eagleton was not as comprehensive as it should have been and Senator Eagleton neglected to mention several hospitalizations for depression.

When McGovern finally was made aware of Senator Eagleton's medical past, he ultimately decided to tap a different running mate three months before the election. As his first set of choices did not agree to run with him, he finally chose Sargent Shriver.

## November 8, 1972

*I never really knew Senator McGovern very well, but was he the best that the Democrats could do? It almost seemed as though everyone felt as though Dick would win again easily and wanted to mark time until the 1976 elections.*

*I have spent some time thinking about the Democratic policies, particular the ones around the social issues like providing social safety nets for people so they have opportunities to succeed even though they may have fallen on difficult times.*

*It seems as though the country needs to take a breather from the passing of a wide swath of social programs before pushing through another. The pendulum of change sees political polities move from one spectrum to the other, in part I believe, to give the country a chance to come to a steady state before initiating another swath of change. If not, the changes may keep the productivity of the country too low to be able to recover quickly.*

*I have gone down this path before in speeches that I have made, and still think that it is an important consideration. The social programs that I was able to start and Lyndon continued (and started more) were a lot for the country to absorb. Fortunately, the economy was strong enough and stable enough for the absorption to be successful.*

*If, however, the changes would have continued or the economy was in a recession, then the foundation for the change would not have been as strong and the changes not as well received. In fact, there is a possibility that trying to implement large changes on weak footing could affect a backfire in public opinion against those policies. Depending on the scope of the backfire, the policies could be set back years, rather than had policy makers waited for the right opportunity.*

*If the perceived power of the leader that happens to be sitting in the White House at the time of recovery is too strong, the inclination to wait for stability may be outweighed by the desire to move forward, possibly leading to short-term success and long-term challenges.*

# Chapter 15 – 1973

On January 22, 1973, the Supreme Court ruled in favor of Roe in the case of Roe v. Wade. They chose to apply the Fourteenth Amendment's clause pertaining to the right of privacy as they felt it applies to the decision of a woman whether or not to terminate her pregnancy.

In their opinion, the Court weighed two competing interests – the protection of the health of the mother, and the viability of the unborn. They defined viability on a sliding scale related to the trimesters of the pregnancy. During the first trimester, they described abortion as being safer than childbirth as the viability of the unborn is not in question. During the first three months, the choice of whether or not to perform an abortion should then be left to the mother and her doctor.

They then went on to say that the State may legislate regarding the application of an abortion prior to the viability of the unborn if the mother's health is at risk for continuing the pregnancy. Finally, the court allowed for abortions during the third trimester only if the mother's health was at risk. Since this initial ruling, the legislation applied to abortion has become less restrictive.

## January 23, 1973

*Abortion is a very difficult social issue. The Supreme Court voted in favor of the constitutionality against abortion bans, but left many questions unanswered. When does life start? Who is responsible for the unborn? When is a child viable? What happens when viability changes? Does religious freedom to be against abortions have any standing?*

*I have no answers. My suggestion for politicians - no comment. Some issues are best addressed by the courts, which is why that branch exists. The politician can then follow the law without speaking against it - one way or the other. One side of the political spectrum will be constantly trying to draw the other into the discussion if they feel they have the side of public opinion, the other will be (or should be) running away.*

*The area that is difficult to run away from is the appointment of judges, particularly at the United States Circuit level or Supreme Court. My suggestion is not to make issues like abortion a primary reason to appoint a justice, but rather more of a hidden agenda, if that is possible. Playing to the crowd in the case of pro-abortion versus anti-abortion (or pro-life) may not have a solution, as there are no clear winners.*

On January 27, 1973, the Paris Peace Accords agreement was signed by the United States, North Vietnam, South Vietnam, and the Provisional Revolutionary Government, an organization comprised of South Vietnamese revolutionaries.

The signing of this agreement signaled the end of the United States' direct involvement in the Vietnam War and the one-way ticket home for the remaining United States troops.

The United States' position in the war had been deteriorating for years. To add insult to injury, after Nixon left office in disgrace and even though promises were made to the South Vietnamese to replace their armament, the Democrat-led Congress exercised the power of the purse and did not appropriate adequate funding to support that equipment replacement for the South Vietnamese. This removal of the United States support quickly led to the final downfall of South Vietnam.

## January 28, 1973

*It is finally over for the United States. Had I known the fate of the United States involvement in the Vietnam War and my fate, I would have stopped our involvement in my first year in office. There were too many lives lost and too many families affected. Too many men who came back to a disrespectful country. Moreover, we lost a war that was likely not winnable from the start.*

*My hat is off to Dick for achieving the result of bringing our troops home as part of the negotiations in Paris.*

## April 12, 1973

*I was joking with Frank today. I asked him who could they possibly have gotten to be the double for Nixon. He is certainly a one-of-a-kind. Bob Hope may be able to pull off the nose. The first thing that the decoy would need to be able to figure out is to determine when and when not to use a razor.*

*It is interesting that I ended up in Dick's state. Not that I am complaining. I do not miss the New England winters. However, I do miss the leaves changing and the variations from season to season. Although, Southern California is a great place to live. I can see why so many people want to live here. The weather is consistent and hardly any rain. It is hard to remember sometimes what month it is. Between the changing seasons and the political cycles, I never had a problem knowing exactly where we were in the calendar.*

*Dick's choice for Vice-President is as suspect as mine. One of the things that you need to do as an administrator is to surround yourself with competent, capable people that you respect to take on their assignments with the passion those assignments require.*

*I suppose being a good administrator is a good rationale for Governors generally making better Presidents. The administrative lessons they learn are difficult to replicate by Senators or Representatives that have little to no experience in running something besides their offices, which is normally not a difficult thing to do. The press does not attack a Senator's chief of staff as they go after a President's choice of Secretary of State.*

*Senators choose running mates and cabinet positions with the next election in mind. Governors seem to be more inclined to choose those in the inner circle that are capable and competent to get the job done. Their inner circles ARE the cabinet members. Inner circles for Senators are political choices and may be selected for the wrong reasons.*

*Occasionally, a fellow like Eisenhower comes along - a built-in leader. A General is an administrator who knows how to surround himself with the best people. People surrounding the leader are needed to save the leader's neck when it needs to be saved. The leader also needs to be excellent at the execution of duties. The catch twenty-two of this is that while Generals may make the best Presidents (starting with General Washington), they typically have developed a large aversion to politics because they have experienced the ability of politicians to get in the way of a smooth execution of wartime campaigns - the blurring of talk and action.*

On October 10, 1973, Vice President Spiro T. Agnew resigned as Vice President to President Nixon. The man who some characterized as Nixon's attack dog, saving the President the negative political image of attacking his opponents, was forced to resign as part of a plea bargain to charges of tax evasion, extortion and conspiracy.

The charges originated in Agnew's home state of Maryland where he served as governor from 1967 to 1969. Agnew was accused of accepting at least one hundred thousand dollars in bribes as an elected official, extending into his reign as Vice President.

Agnew's plea bargain allowed him to enter a no contest plea for the charge of tax evasion on the ill-gotten gains in exchange for his resignation as Vice President. With the charges looking over him, Agnew's effectiveness as Nixon attack dog was impacted.

The Twenty-fifth Amendment to the Constitution that was, in part, a result of the shooting in Dallas in 1963, was followed for the first time. Nixon was now in a position to appoint a predecessor to Agnew, choosing Michigan Senator Gerald Ford.

## October 10, 1973

*The resignation of Vice President Agnew may be just a drop in the bucket of the unfolding of Dick's presidency. Had the resignation happened prior to the election, it may have been interesting to see its impact. The result may have not been different because McGovern's candidacy was not gaining any traction, but it may have not been a landslide.*

*Historians may continue to compare my Presidency with others. As it relates to Dick, one of the things that we seem to have had in common was our inability to choose vice presidents very well. I think he may have done better with his choice from when he ran against me, Henry Cabot Lodge, rather than just using him as an envoy to Rome.*

*Had I to choose all over again, I may have picked Governor Stevenson. Adlai was a good man, even though I am not certain he agreed with many of my policies. He may have been a bit too old for my ticket, but Johnson was no spring chicken. The advantage that Johnson had was his ability to draw some votes in the South. In hindsight a dozen years later, would it not have been interesting had I picked Martin Luther King Jr.? That would have set the party in a tailspin!*

*I gave Adlai a good consolation post, I thought, the appointment as the United States Ambassador to the United Nations.*

# Chapter 16 – 1974

Faced with the strong likelihood of impeachment, on August 9, 1974, Richard Nixon resigned from his post as President of the United States.

During his resignation speech, Nixon spent the majority of his words praising his accomplishments while in office, seemingly in an attempt to mire his legacy in the positives rather than the negatives that led to his resignation.

While Nixon may have not orchestrated or had knowledge of the break-in into Democratic offices at the Watergate hotel, eventually he was involved to some degree in the cover-up, which turned into the focus of the media and resulting pressure to have him removed from office.

### August 9, 1974

*Poor Dick. His desire to know what his 'enemies' are up to caught up with him. Had he not covered it up and given his detractors an opportunity to peek more under the covers, he may have been able to avoid the humiliation of resigning from the*

*Presidency. He is certainly not the first President that probably should have resigned for activities uncharacteristic of a President, nor will he likely be the last.*

*It reminds me of college sports. It is the responsibility of colleges to turn out graduates that are ready to be participating members of society. Otherwise, it is not worth the investment. Prospective students have the opportunity to get a college education largely paid for because of their participation in college athletics. However, college athletics seems to be getting more lucrative in the money that is generated at the gate, by endorsements, and by television. As there is more money involved, and the resulting power of the additional money, the temptation of getting involved in activities that are unbecoming of athletics becomes increasingly strong.*

*Politics is similar. As government becomes bigger and stronger, the pressure to maintain control of that power is increasingly strong. Working with Congress is challenging enough, but when the power shifts from the left to the right like a pendulum, there is motivation to maintain control so you do not lose perceived ground that you have gained. Thus, people tend to do things that they normally may not do in order to maintain that power - to freeze the pendulum in place on your side of the thinking. Armchair quarterbacking is easy from where I am sitting, but it seems to me as though you cannot keep the pendulum on one side too long. Sir Isaac Newton would likely say that the force of gravity would eventually pull the pendulum down and toward the center before it may swing the other direction. If the velocity of the swing in the opposite direction is high, there is a good likelihood that the pendulum may swing to the other direction further that where it started.*

On September 8, 1974, President Ford pardoned former President Richard Nixon for any crimes he may have committed as President during the Watergate Scandal. Some say this was the most controversial act that President Ford did during his presidency.

It was only a little more than one month into Ford's presidency when he absolved the former President of any wrongdoing to prevent a potential circus of courtroom proceedings involving a former President.

The possible impending indictment was a charge of obstruction of justice concerning the Watergate breaking and wiretapping of the Democratic National Headquarters at the Watergate hotel in Washington DC.

It is interesting to reflect on the huge media focus on the obstruction of justice and associated cover-ups that happened in the early 1970's. As the next four decades unraveled, Presidential obstructions of justice seemed to become more commonplace with less media attention. One could project the cover-ups of Presidential obstructions in years hence to the media themselves – the media that once were the bulldogs of seeking the truth.

## September 12, 1974

*Twenty-one years ago this week, Jackie and I were married. I wish I was there for Jackie, Caroline and John and was there as they grew. I know how divorced men must feel when they lose access to their children. It hurts, every day not being there for them and living their youth with them. I appreciate all that Jackie has done for our children and hope that she never finds out that I survived that day in Dallas.*

# Chapter 17 – 1975

Aristotle Socrates Onassis died on March 15, 1975 of a respiratory failure after only seven and a half years of marriage to Jackie. While she did not receive a substantial portion of his huge fortune, she was certainly taken care of.

Jackie lived well while she was married to Aristotle. If they were not at her apartment in New York City or her horse farm in New Jersey, they were at his house in Athens, apartment in Paris or his island in Greece (Skorpios). Of course, they could also be seen on his 325-foot yacht "Christine" named after his beloved daughter who inherited 55% of his fortune.

### March 16, 1975

*I just heard that Aristotle Onassis died. Jackie cannot catch a break. The fortunate aspect of her marriage to Onassis is the she was protected at a time when she and the children needed it the most.*

On April 30, 1975, North Vietnam's People's Army of Vietnam and the Viet Cong captured Saigon, the capital of South Vietnam. With promised support from the United States being cut off, partially because Nixon, who made the promise, was no longer in office, the fate of South Vietnam was inevitable. Soon after the fall of the capital, South Vietnam surrendered which officially ended the Vietnam War.

## May 1, 1975

*Three months after the United States ended involvement in the Vietnam War, Saigon was taken over by the North Vietnamese. The Vietnam War is over and with any luck, we learn from our mistakes. First lesson - joining in on a regional conflict is going to be difficult to succeed and difficult to maintain the support of the American people. Second lesson - once we leave, the side that we were not supporting will eventually, and in this case quickly, lose.*

*Understanding history and being able to use those lessons learned while making decisions about current events is likely difficult, but important. The manipulators of history use the past to lay out the map of manipulations. Leaders must also use history to counter the influence of those detractors otherwise will be destined to repeat the errors of the past.*

## July 1, 1975

*I hear a lot of talk about relationships between Marilyn Monroe and me. Let me put these suppositions to rest, Marilyn and I never had an affair. I pledged my faithfulness to Jackie, and I followed through with that promise. Yes, Marilyn was very flirty around me. It is very possible that she would have wanted an affair, but it never happened. I always thought she liked Bobby better.*

*However, I am not sure Bobby would have strayed either. Not because an affair may go public and possibly ruin our political careers. No, the major force that was keeping us faithful was our Mother. There were many things in our lives that she was not happy with, but gave us enough line that we could swim around freely in the pond. However, we all knew that with one flick of her wrist, the hook would set in our cheek and we would be yanked out of the pond.*

# Chapter 18 – 1976

July 4, 1976 marked the two hundredth anniversary of the United States, celebrated with a countrywide Bicentennial celebration.

Many celebrations and events marked the bicentennial milestone. Events included; the reverse of coins were temporarily reminted and the American Freedom train toured the forty-eight contiguous States, travelling over twenty-five thousand miles, and President Ford hosted a visit by England's Queen Elizabeth II.

### July 4, 1976

*Today is an important day in the history of the United States. It is the day that we declared our independence from the tyrannical rule of the King of England and told the world that we were ready to set our small ship to sail into the future on our own power and with the navigational charts of documents such as the Constitution, Declaration of Independence and the Bill of Rights. I take this day to collect my thoughts about the key navigational chart, the Constitution, and reflect on what it means to me today.*

129

     <u>*Preamble*</u> *"We the People of the United States, in Order to form a more perfect Union, establish Justice, insure domestic Tranquility, provide for the common defence, promote the general Welfare, and secure the Blessings of Liberty to ourselves and our Posterity, do ordain and establish this Constitution for the United States of America."*

     *The preamble to the constitution throws down the challenge to the people. This challenge is related to my analogy of rock/paper/scissors because it is compelling us to strike a balance among many ideas and develop common goals. As I see it, the preamble contains five main challenges to the people of the United States, five areas that when addressed in a holistic manner make sense as common goals for all and can result in a more perfect union. However, when they are allowed to splinter, and be addressed as individual rocks or paper or scissors, then they will compete against each other, become divisive, and the union is less perfect.*

     <u>*Justice*</u> *is first and aligns with the notion that we are a nation of laws and no one should be above the law. However, if laws become too restrictive, they can interfere in liberties of individuals.*

     *For example, since the turn of the century, Americans have enjoyed the ability to climb into a car and drive around the country freely and as they see fit. All you need is a license to drive in the State in which you live and a tank full of gasoline. Imagine if each State decided that it wanted to know when someone from another State was entering the State and, to keep track, had someone at the border writing down license plates of out-of-state vehicles.*

     *Citizens may feel as if there is an overstepping of State governments' power and that their liberties of freedom of travel are being infringed upon. Even though the rationale for the State conducting this surveillance may be helpful in catching criminals, the outcome must be weighed with the means to get to that outcome.*

*Domestic tranquility focuses on our ability to work together. States need to be able to work together and, while they can compete for resources, they should do so in an organized and civil way. The interactions between counties and parishes within each State should work together similarly as it is up to the individual States to ensure its own internal domestic tranquility. Finally, one of the biggest challenges is the extent that government needs to provide the opportunity for domestic tranquility without interfering with the rights of the States to manage their own tranquility.*

*Common defense is one of the more basic challenges. In the case of the Constitutional reference, defense refers to the defense against foreign entities. Intrastate defense should be covered by the challenge of domestic tranquility. The collective strength of all States contributing to a federal composite defense structure is typically universally understood. However, the priority of investment in the common defense versus other initiatives seems to have vacillated from administration to administration and need to need.*

*Promotion of general welfare is at least as important as a common defense. In order for Americans to have opportunities, there needs to be a basic level of standards for areas such as education, health, safety, housing, and financial stability. Promotion of these areas can be seen as at least a two-fold endeavor. First, promotion can be just a cheerleader, but also can be a driver. Establishment of the infrastructure can be accomplished at the State level, but could be difficult to create and maintain a baseline level of support at the State level and needs to be supplemented at the Federal level.*

*Promotion also means that the basic level of common welfare should constantly be improved. As the bar rises, and common welfare continually is modified, resources need to be available to support it. The challenge with maintaining a common level of general welfare is that it can interfere with the liberties and pursuits of others. This balance is another area that swings from more on the liberal interpretation to the conservative. I believe that it is a matter of priorities and what the country can afford to do. Priorities change as the environment changes, both domestic and foreign. Legislators and administrators need to weigh all factors before deciding what the priorities should be and not totally rely on historical policy or political planks.*

**Article 1, Section 1** **"All legislative Powers herein granted shall be vested in a Congress of the United States, which shall consist of a Senate and House of Representatives."**

*The division of Congress into two houses, one that provides equality to each State and one that is representative of the people has served the country well in making changes deliberate and meaningful. It has also aided the acceptance of changes by the public.*

**Article 1, Section 2** **"The House of Representatives shall be composed of Members chosen every second Year by the People of the several States, and the Electors in each State shall have the Qualifications requisite for Electors of the most numerous Branch of the State Legislature.**

**No Person shall be a Representative who shall not have attained to the Age of twenty five Years, and been seven Years a Citizen of the United States, and who shall not, when elected, be an Inhabitant of that State in which he shall be chosen.**

**Representatives and direct Taxes shall be apportioned among the several States which may be included within this Union, according to their respective Numbers, which shall be determined by adding to the whole Number of free Persons, including those bound to Service for a Term of Years, and excluding Indians not taxed, three**

*fifths of all other Persons. The actual Enumeration shall be made within three Years after the first Meeting of the Congress of the United States, and within every subsequent Term of ten Years, in such Manner as they shall by Law direct. The Number of Representatives shall not exceed one for every thirty Thousand, but each State shall have at Least one Representative; and until such enumeration shall be made, the State of New Hampshire shall be entitled to chuse three, Massachusetts eight, Rhode-Island and Providence Plantations one, Connecticut five, New-York six, New Jersey four, Pennsylvania eight, Delaware one, Maryland six, Virginia ten, North Carolina five, South Carolina five, and Georgia three.*

*When vacancies happen in the Representation from any State, the Executive Authority thereof shall issue Writs of Election to fill such Vacancies.*

*The House of Representatives shall chuse their Speaker and other Officers; and shall have the sole Power of Impeachment."*

*The founders knew they needed financial support from the people to be able to carry out Federal initiatives designed to support the people as a whole. One of the issues that revolutionaries had with King George was the fact that the people in America were being taxed and not being fairly represented by those that were spending their money.*

*The founders of the country realized that if people do not have representation aligned with the assessed amount of tax burden that misalignment could result in an imbalance of power. If those paying taxes are not equally represented, then there is a likelihood that the representative power would be shifted to those that pay disproportionally less in taxes and could cause higher assessments to those paying, reducing their motivation to participate.*

*The concept of taxation without representation was so strong, that the writers and approvers of the Constitution included the right to impose taxes and the establishment of a model of representation in the same paragraph.*

    *Article 1, Section 3* *"The Senate of the United States shall be composed of two Senators from each State, chosen by the Legislature thereof for six Years; and each Senator shall have one Vote.*

    *Immediately after they shall be assembled in Consequence of the first Election, they shall be divided as equally as may be into three Classes. The Seats of the Senators of the first Class shall be vacated at the Expiration of the second Year, of the second Class at the Expiration of the fourth Year, and of the third Class at the Expiration of the sixth Year, so that one third may be chosen every second Year; and if Vacancies happen by Resignation, or otherwise, during the Recess of the Legislature of any State, the Executive thereof may make temporary Appointments until the next Meeting of the Legislature, which shall then fill such Vacancies.*

    *No Person shall be a Senator who shall not have attained to the Age of thirty Years, and been nine Years a Citizen of the United States, and who shall not, when elected, be an Inhabitant of that State for which he shall be chosen.*

    *The Vice President of the United States shall be President of the Senate, but shall have no Vote, unless they be equally divided.*

    *The Senate shall chuse their other Officers, and also a President pro tempore, in the Absence of the Vice President, or when he shall exercise the Office of President of the United States.*

    *The Senate shall have the sole Power to try all Impeachments. When sitting for that Purpose, they shall be on Oath or Affirmation. When the President of the United States is tried, the Chief Justice shall preside: And no Person shall be convicted without the Concurrence of two thirds of the Members present.*

*Judgment in Cases of Impeachment shall not extend further than to removal from Office, and disqualification to hold and enjoy any Office of honor, Trust or Profit under the United States: but the Party convicted shall nevertheless be liable and subject to Indictment, Trial, Judgment and Punishment, according to Law."*

This section of the Constitution establishes the creation of the Senate, which rather than being representatives of the people of the entire United States as is the House of Representative, the Senate is established to represent the States. Each State is given two votes in the Senate.

It was also assumed by the founders that Senators would be the more distinguished group in Congress. They set the minimum age for being a member of the House at twenty-five but raised that minimum age for Senators to thirty.

The House was set forth as the body responsible for impeachment, which is the identification of wrongdoing based on the articles of impeachment. The Senate then, is charged with the final vote on removal from office.

This provision can be described as a form of shunning, commonly used as punishment by many religious entities. While not a civil punishment it is more of a social punishment where the Congress essentially turns their backs toward the shunned/impeached individual and does not allow them "to hold and enjoy any Office of honor, Trust or Profit under the United States."

*Article 1, Section 4* *"The Times, Places and Manner of holding Elections for Senators and Representatives, shall be prescribed in each State by the Legislature thereof; but the Congress may at any time by Law make or alter such Regulations, except as to the Places of chusing Senators.*

*The Congress shall assemble at least once in every Year, and such Meeting shall be on the first Monday in December, unless they shall by Law appoint a different Day."*

*Sandwiching the assembly of Congress between Thanksgiving and Christmas may have been a bit shortsighted as the distance from Washington D.C. to newly forming States became greater without the assistance of air travel.*

*However, imagine the lack of fodder for political pundits if Congress was only in session for a couple weeks in December.*

*Making the States responsible for elections was generally a good idea, except when issues of social injustices arise like allowing women to vote. In those cases, the government needs to step in to enforce individual rights.*

<u>*Article 1, Section 5*</u> *"Each House shall be the Judge of the Elections, Returns and Qualifications of its own Members, and a Majority of each shall constitute a Quorum to do Business; but a smaller Number may adjourn from day to day, and may be authorized to compel the Attendance of absent Members, in such Manner, and under such Penalties as each House may provide.*

*Each House may determine the Rules of its Proceedings, punish its Members for disorderly Behaviour, and, with the Concurrence of two thirds, expel a Member.*

*Each House shall keep a Journal of its Proceedings, and from time to time publish the same, excepting such Parts as may in their Judgment require Secrecy; and the Yeas and Nays of the Members of either House on any question shall, at the Desire of one fifth of those Present, be entered on the Journal.*

*Neither House, during the Session of Congress, shall, without the Consent of the other, adjourn for more than three days, nor to any other Place than that in which the two Houses shall be sitting."*

*The authors of the Constitution wanted to maintain transparency to the deliberations and activities of each house of Congress. The transparency enumerated in the areas that were seen as important at the time such as how the votes are recorded and a journal of all proceedings.*

*It is also interesting to note the fact that the House and Senate need to know what each other is doing. While in session, they are not permitted to adjourn for more than three days without the approval of the other congressional body. Nor are they allowed to officially meet in a location that keeps them apart.*

**<u>Article 1, Section 6</u> "The Senators and Representatives shall receive a Compensation for their Services, to be ascertained by Law, and paid out of the Treasury of the United States. They shall in all Cases, except Treason, Felony and Breach of the Peace, be privileged from Arrest during their Attendance at the Session of their respective Houses, and in going to and returning from the same; and for any Speech or Debate in either House, they shall not be questioned in any other Place.**

**No Senator or Representative shall, during the Time for which he was elected, be appointed to any civil Office under the Authority of the United States, which shall have been created, or the Emoluments whereof shall have been encreased during such time; and no Person holding any Office under the United States, shall be a Member of either House during his Continuance in Office."**

*Senators and Representatives are encouraged to be free to speak and participate in their respective House without retribution, either within the confines of the session or to and from. To avoid a conflict of interest, they are not allowed to hold an office other than the House or Senate seat to which they were elected.*

*Affiliation with entities outside of their elected office was seen by Constitutional authors as potentially being in conflict with their duties to represent the people or States to which they are obliged.*

*My perception is that these affiliations have atrophied over time. There are a number of 'distractors' in Washington D.C. that pull members' focus away from the representation of the people and the States toward special interests whose wheels may be squeakier than the electorate. I encourage office holders periodically to reassess their success in actually representing the views of the constituency to which they are bound.*

**<u>Article 1, Section 7</u> "All Bills for raising Revenue shall originate in the House of Representatives; but the Senate may propose or concur with Amendments as on other Bills.**

**Every Bill which shall have passed the House of Representatives and the Senate, shall, before it become a Law, be presented to the President of the United States: If he approve he shall sign it, but if not he shall return it, with his Objections to that House in which it shall have originated, who shall enter the Objections at large on their Journal, and proceed to reconsider it. If after such Reconsideration two thirds of that House shall agree to pass the Bill, it shall be sent, together with the Objections, to the other House, by which it shall likewise be reconsidered, and if approved by two thirds of that House, it shall become a Law. But in all such Cases the Votes of both Houses shall be determined by yeas and Nays, and the Names of the Persons voting for and against the Bill shall be entered on the Journal of each House respectively. If any Bill shall not be returned by the President within ten Days (Sundays excepted) after it shall have been presented to him, the Same shall be a Law, in like Manner as if he had signed**

*it, unless the Congress by their Adjournment prevent its Return, in which Case it shall not be a Law.*

*Every Order, Resolution, or Vote to which the Concurrence of the Senate and House of Representatives may be necessary (except on a question of Adjournment) shall be presented to the President of the United States; and before the Same shall take Effect, shall be approved by him, or being disapproved by him, shall be repassed by two thirds of the Senate and House of Representatives, according to the Rules and Limitations prescribed in the Case of a Bill."*

*This is a relative simple article, but not always the easiest to maneuver. It sets forth the idea that laws that spend money originate in the House, but the Senate must concur. This is to give the people and the States equal representation as spending bills may impact either and may be mutually exclusive. Then, of course, Presidential signature is required for passage unless there is a two-thirds majority of Congress to override.*

*Article 1, Section 8* *"The Congress shall have Power To lay and collect Taxes, Duties, Imposts and Excises, to pay the Debts and provide for the common Defence and general Welfare of the United States; but all Duties, Imposts and Excises shall be uniform throughout the United States;*

*To borrow Money on the credit of the United States;*

*To regulate Commerce with foreign Nations, and among the several States, and with the Indian Tribes;*

*To establish an uniform Rule of Naturalization, and uniform Laws on the subject of Bankruptcies throughout the United States;*

*To coin Money, regulate the Value thereof, and of foreign Coin, and fix the Standard of Weights and Measures;*

*To provide for the Punishment of counterfeiting the Securities and current Coin of the United States;*

*To establish Post Offices and post Roads;*

*To promote the Progress of Science and useful Arts, by securing for limited Times to Authors and Inventors the exclusive Right to their respective Writings and Discoveries;*

*To constitute Tribunals inferior to the supreme Court;*

*To define and punish Piracies and Felonies committed on the high Seas, and Offences against the Law of Nations;*

*To declare War, grant Letters of Marque and Reprisal, and make Rules concerning Captures on Land and Water;*

*To raise and support Armies, but no Appropriation of Money to that Use shall be for a longer Term than two Years;*

*To provide and maintain a Navy;*

*To make Rules for the Government and Regulation of the land and naval Forces;*

*To provide for calling forth the Militia to execute the Laws of the Union, suppress Insurrections and repel Invasions;*

*To provide for organizing, arming, and disciplining, the Militia, and for governing such Part of them as may be employed in the Service of the United States, reserving to the States respectively, the Appointment of the Officers, and the Authority of training the Militia according to the discipline prescribed by Congress;*

*To exercise exclusive Legislation in all Cases whatsoever, over such District (not exceeding ten Miles square) as may, by Cession of particular States, and the Acceptance of Congress, become the Seat of the Government of the United States, and to exercise like Authority over all Places purchased by the Consent of the Legislature of the State in which the Same shall be, for the Erection of Forts,*

*Magazines, Arsenals, dock-Yards, and other needful Buildings;--And*

*To make all Laws which shall be necessary and proper for carrying into Execution the foregoing Powers, and all other Powers vested by this Constitution in the Government of the United States, or in any Department or Officer thereof."*

*The clause in the beginning of this article is interesting, as it demands that duties (taxes on things), imposts (taxes on imports) and excises (like gasoline tax or cigarette tax) be uniform throughout the United States. The fact that there is no mention of personal tax in the list has left interpretation open to the progressive tax system.*

*Of the fifteen main subsections of this article, seven deal with the military, five deal with banking-related topics, one for the post office, one for copyrights and protections for inventors, and one for courts. This focus makes it clear what was on the minds of the framers of the Constitution. There is nothing I have read that dealt with imposing a common national speed limit for highways. Of course, at the time of its writing, horses could only go so fast.*

*The first subsection states that Congress can borrow money on United States credit. As with citizens of the United States, borrowing is cheaper when credit is good. We must strive to keep the credit of the United States strong to lessen additional costs to the citizens. As with citizens, avoiding excess borrowing that passes debt to children and grandchildren is not a sound policy.*

*The next subsection grants Congress the ability to regulate trade with other countries, among the States and with Indians. Even though the initial focus has been stretched through the years, the need to make certain there is freedom of trade from one State to the next is important from a commerce standpoint to work together to form a more perfect union rather than a hodgepodge of pieces.*

*The third subsection grants Congress the authority to control immigration and create common nationwide laws pertaining to bankruptcies.*

*The next subsection allows Congress to create money that has a nationwide uniform value. It also grants Congress the power to determine the standard of weights and measures, which interestingly is still the standard used by England when the Constitution was written. The following subsection is related as it allows for punishment of counterfeiting of United States money.*

*Post roads are the roads that the post office used to distribute the mail, which falls under the scope of Congressional purview along with the establishment of a common postal system.*

*The writers of the Constitution wanted to encourage the free creation of new additions to the Arts and Sciences. One of the ways to do so is to protect creations and inventions through rights of copy, which prevents the unauthorized use of those creations and discoveries.*

*The next subsection allows Congress to create a court system that feeds through to the Supreme Court.*

*The Law of Nations was a philosophy written about by Emerich de Vattel (I had to look up his name). This philosophy was set forth over two hundred years ago and focused on the need for nations to work together, particularly when developing laws that affect all nations. The best example of this in the 1750's was maritime law, thus the focus on piracy.*

*Letters of Marque and Reprisal is essentially a way to deputize someone to be able to capture enemy ships and bring them to court. Almost like a bounty hunter. In addition to the ability to charter bounty hunters, the Congress can declare war and determine what to do with detainees of war.*

*The next five sub articles provide power to Congress specific to defense, foreign and domestic. Specific branches enumerated are; Army (with no more than a two year funding provision before needing to seek funding again), Navy, Army and*

*Navy governance, foreign and domestic Militia, and Militia governance.*

*The last two sub articles establish the federalization of land for the District of Columbia for the capital and provide for Congress' ability to establish laws pertaining to the enumerated powers of this Article 1, Section 8.*

**Article 1, Section 9** *"The Migration or Importation of such Persons as any of the States now existing shall think proper to admit, shall not be prohibited by the Congress prior to the Year one thousand eight hundred and eight, but a Tax or duty may be imposed on such Importation, not exceeding ten dollars for each Person.*

*The Privilege of the Writ of Habeas Corpus shall not be suspended, unless when in Cases of Rebellion or Invasion the public Safety may require it.*

*No Bill of Attainder or ex post facto Law shall be passed.*

*No Capitation, or other direct, Tax shall be laid, unless in Proportion to the Census or enumeration herein before directed to be taken.*

*No Tax or Duty shall be laid on Articles exported from any State.*

*No Preference shall be given by any Regulation of Commerce or Revenue to the Ports of one State over those of another; nor shall Vessels bound to, or from, one State, be obliged to enter, clear, or pay Duties in another.*

*No Money shall be drawn from the Treasury, but in Consequence of Appropriations made by Law; and a regular Statement and Account of the Receipts and Expenditures of all public Money shall be published from time to time.*

*No Title of Nobility shall be granted by the United States: And no Person holding any Office of Profit or Trust under them, shall, without the Consent of the Congress, accept of any present, Emolument, Office, or Title, of any kind whatever, from any King, Prince, or foreign State."*

This article is an interesting hodgepodge of issues that the founders determined to be important to enumerate. They warrant discussion one at a time.

The first item pertains to immigration. The founders knew that they needed to allow for the growth of the States. The first round of immigration, which was to be followed until 1808, allowed for the States to choose who to admit into their States with a maximum admittance price of ten dollars per person.

The second item pertains to the ability to bring a possible offender before a court as long as it does not interfere with public safety.

The third item is pragmatic, as it does not allow anyone to create a law against something that has already happened. This makes in incumbent on lawmakers to think about all possible ways a law can be broken and include them in the laws that are written, which sometimes results in a lot of words in each law.

Capitation is a uniform tax. This subsection states that all uniform taxation must be proportionate within the overall population of the United States. Proportionate as a property tax based on the value of your property or a sales tax based on the value of your purchase.

The next subsection does not allow for additional taxation to a member of another State more than what is being taxed of a member of the original State. This is to help keep commerce flowing freely among the States.

When the United States was in its infancy, one of the most important assets that a State could have is a port to the ocean. A review of the original States on the map shows a State like Pennsylvania that is largely landlocked still has access to the ocean in Philadelphia. A competition among ports between the various States was encouraged as it was seen to foster trade. Additional taxes levied were not allowed.

*The next subsection dealt with the ability of the United States to pay its bills, but only those that were sanctioned by law. It was deemed important for transparency that receipts for expenditures be collected and reported.*

*The final subsection of Section 9 was directed toward the fear that any one person would attain the power of someone like King George. Therefore, no one that works for the government, like a president, can take a title like "King". Nor can a foreign country grant a similar title, unless Congress agrees.*

**_Article 1, Section 10_** **"No State shall enter into any Treaty, Alliance, or Confederation; grant Letters of Marque and Reprisal; coin Money; emit Bills of Credit; make any Thing but gold and silver Coin a Tender in Payment of Debts; pass any Bill of Attainder, ex post facto Law, or Law impairing the Obligation of Contracts, or grant any Title of Nobility.**

**No State shall, without the Consent of the Congress, lay any Imposts or Duties on Imports or Exports, except what may be absolutely necessary for executing it's inspection Laws: and the net Produce of all Duties and Imposts, laid by any State on Imports or Exports, shall be for the Use of the Treasury of the United States; and all such Laws shall be subject to the Revision and Controul of the Congress.**

**No State shall, without the Consent of Congress, lay any Duty of Tonnage, keep Troops, or Ships of War in time of Peace, enter into any Agreement or Compact with another State, or with a foreign Power, or engage in War, unless actually invaded, or in such imminent Danger as will not admit of delay."**

*The final section of Article 1 of the Constitution tells the States that they are not allowed to exercise power in any of the areas that are set forth to be controlled at the Federal level, serving as a bit of summary for Article 1.*

*Article II, Section 1* "*The executive Power shall be vested in a President of the United States of America. He shall hold his Office during the Term of four Years, and, together with the Vice President, chosen for the same Term, be elected, as follows:*

*Each State shall appoint, in such Manner as the Legislature thereof may direct, a Number of Electors, equal to the whole Number of Senators and Representatives to which the State may be entitled in the Congress: but no Senator or Representative, or Person holding an Office of Trust or Profit under the United States, shall be appointed an Elector.*

*The Electors shall meet in their respective States, and vote by Ballot for two Persons, of whom one at least shall not be an Inhabitant of the same State with themselves. And they shall make a List of all the Persons voted for, and of the Number of Votes for each; which List they shall sign and certify, and transmit sealed to the Seat of the Government of the United States, directed to the President of the Senate. The President of the Senate shall, in the Presence of the Senate and House of Representatives, open all the Certificates, and the Votes shall then be counted. The Person having the greatest Number of Votes shall be the President, if such Number be a Majority of the whole Number of Electors appointed; and if there be more than one who have such Majority, and have an equal Number of Votes, then the House of Representatives shall immediately chuse by Ballot one of them for President; and if no Person have a Majority, then from the five highest on the List the said House shall in like Manner chuse the President. But in chusing the President, the Votes shall be taken by States, the Representation from each State having one Vote; A quorum for this purpose shall consist of a Member or Members from two thirds of the States, and a*

*Majority of all the States shall be necessary to a Choice. In every Case, after the Choice of the President, the Person having the greatest Number of Votes of the Electors shall be the Vice President. But if there should remain two or more who have equal Votes, the Senate shall chuse from them by Ballot the Vice President.*

*The Congress may determine the Time of chusing the Electors, and the Day on which they shall give their Votes; which Day shall be the same throughout the United States.*

*No Person except a natural born Citizen, or a Citizen of the United States, at the time of the Adoption of this Constitution, shall be eligible to the Office of President; neither shall any Person be eligible to that Office who shall not have attained to the Age of thirty five Years, and been fourteen Years a Resident within the United States.*

*In Case of the Removal of the President from Office, or of his Death, Resignation, or Inability to discharge the Powers and Duties of the said Office, the Same shall devolve on the Vice President, and the Congress may by Law provide for the Case of Removal, Death, Resignation or Inability, both of the President and Vice President, declaring what Officer shall then act as President, and such Officer shall act accordingly, until the Disability be removed, or a President shall be elected.*

*The President shall, at stated Times, receive for his Services, a Compensation, which shall neither be increased nor diminished during the Period for which he shall have been elected, and he shall not receive within that Period any other Emolument from the United States, or any of them.*

*Before he enter on the Execution of his Office, he shall take the following Oath or Affirmation:--"I do solemnly swear (or affirm) that I will faithfully execute the Office of President of the United States, and will to the best of my Ability, preserve, protect and defend the Constitution of the United States."*

While Article 1 focuses primarily on governance and the powers of Congress, Article II focuses on the powers of the President. Members of Congress should memorize Article I, the President and Vice President should memorize Article II.

The first sub section of Section 1 sets the term of office of the President at four years. When I first studied the Federal government as a teenager, I was confused by the varied terms of the House, Senate and President. However, as I got older, the varying terms made a lot of sense. The House is two years so there can be a rotation of representatives, keeping the will of the people at the forefront of the thinking of their representative. The Senate is six years, which provides them an opportunity for a Senator to get to know the needs of the State that Senator is representing more and be better able to respond. The President's term is in the middle – four years. Every two years, all House members' seats are up for grabs and one third of the Senate. Every other two-year period, the Presidential election is part of the mix.

When the Constitution was written, life expectancy had not changed much for much of history, as the writers knew it. The average person's expectation was to live up to about fifty years. Now, people expect to live twenty to thirty years longer than that. That is many extra terms that the founders did not contemplate would be served.

The second sub section establishes the make-up of electors of the President, setting up for the Electoral College. An important part of being an elector is that you cannot be a Representative or a Senator.

The next sub section describes the process the Electoral College must follow to select the President. Essentially, they get together in their State, vote for the President (and Vice-President when the document was written) and send their ballot to the President of the Senate. The Senate makes sense over the House because there will typically be two thirds of them that did not just

148

*go through the election process. In the Senate, the votes are tallied and a winner is certified. If there is a tie, the House of Representatives is called on and a majority vote chooses the President. This is why they cannot also be on the Electoral College.*

*The next sub section gives Congress the power to set a single election day for all the states at once.*

*The next sub section describes the qualifications for President – at least thirty-five years old, naturalized citizen, and at least fourteen years living in the United States.*

*The final three subsections cover the removal of the President from office, the President's compensation, and the text of the Presidential oath of office where the President elect states an affirmation to preserve, protect and defend the Constitution. If they do not memorize Article II, Presidents should at least memorize their oath of office.*

**<u>Article II, Section 2</u> "The President shall be Commander in Chief of the Army and Navy of the United States, and of the Militia of the several States, when called into the actual Service of the United States; he may require the Opinion, in writing, of the principal Officer in each of the executive Departments, upon any Subject relating to the Duties of their respective Offices, and he shall have Power to grant Reprieves and Pardons for Offences against the United States, except in Cases of Impeachment.**

**He shall have Power, by and with the Advice and Consent of the Senate, to make Treaties, provided two thirds of the Senators present concur; and he shall nominate, and by and with the Advice and Consent of the Senate, shall appoint Ambassadors, other public Ministers and Consuls, Judges of the supreme Court, and all other Officers of the United States, whose Appointments are not herein otherwise provided for, and which shall be established by Law: but the Congress may by Law vest the**

*Appointment of such inferior Officers, as they think proper, in the President alone, in the Courts of Law, or in the Heads of Departments.*

*The President shall have Power to fill up all Vacancies that may happen during the Recess of the Senate, by granting Commissions which shall expire at the End of their next Session."*

Section 2 grants the President the power over the armed services as Commander in Chief. The President initiates the process of entering into treaties with foreign governments and two-thirds agreement by the Senate. The President also appoints judges and other high-level public officials. For those that require consent of Congress, the President may make appointments during Senate recess with the understanding that those appointments expire at the end of the next Senate session.

**<u>Article II, Section 3</u>  "He shall from time to time give to the Congress Information of the State of the Union, and recommend to their Consideration such Measures as he shall judge necessary and expedient; he may, on extraordinary Occasions, convene both Houses, or either of them, and in Case of Disagreement between them, with Respect to the Time of Adjournment, he may adjourn them to such Time as he shall think proper; he shall receive Ambassadors and other public Ministers; he shall take Care that the Laws be faithfully executed, and shall Commission all the Officers of the United States."**

Section 3 allows the President to give a State of the Union address in front of both houses. The President can occasionally convene Congress if necessary; receive foreign diplomats, and commission officers of the armed forces.

**<u>Article II, Section 4</u>  "The President, Vice President and all civil Officers of the United States, shall be removed**

*from Office on Impeachment for, and Conviction of,*
*Treason, Bribery, or other high Crimes and Misdemeanors."*

High crimes and misdemeanors are somewhat of a broad definition of what it takes a President to be impeached. In addition to treason and bribery, it includes refusal to obey a lawful order, dereliction of duty, failure to supervise, misuse of assets, intimidation, abuse of authority, perjury of oath, and conduct unbecoming of the President of the United States.

Perhaps with the impeachment of Dick, future presidents will see that they stay above the fray and remember the definition of high crimes and misdemeanors to avoid the reality or perception that they have strayed.


*Article III, Section 1* **"The judicial Power of the**
**United States shall be vested in one supreme Court, and in**
**such inferior Courts as the Congress may from time to time**
**ordain and establish. The Judges, both of the supreme and**
**inferior Courts, shall hold their Offices during good**
**Behaviour, and shall, at stated Times, receive for their**
**Services a Compensation, which shall not be diminished**
**during their Continuance in Office."**

The first section of Article III covers the third branch of government, the Supreme Court. It basically allows for the creation of the Supreme Court and inferior courts and ensures they are paid.


*Article III, Section 2* **"The judicial Power shall**
**extend to all Cases, in Law and Equity, arising under this**
**Constitution, the Laws of the United States, and Treaties**
**made, or which shall be made, under their Authority;--to all**
**Cases affecting Ambassadors, other public Ministers and**
**Consuls;--to all Cases of admiralty and maritime**
**Jurisdiction;--to Controversies to which the United States**
**shall be a Party;--to Controversies between two or more**
**States;-- between a State and Citizens of another State,--**

*between Citizens of different States,--between Citizens of the same State claiming Lands under Grants of different States, and between a State, or the Citizens thereof, and foreign States, Citizens or Subjects.*

*In all Cases affecting Ambassadors, other public Ministers and Consuls, and those in which a State shall be Party, the supreme Court shall have original Jurisdiction. In all the other Cases before mentioned, the supreme Court shall have appellate Jurisdiction, both as to Law and Fact, with such Exceptions, and under such Regulations as the Congress shall make.*

*The Trial of all Crimes, except in Cases of Impeachment, shall be by Jury; and such Trial shall be held in the State where the said Crimes shall have been committed; but when not committed within any State, the Trial shall be at such Place or Places as the Congress may by Law have directed."*

Section 2 provides an original jurisdiction for the Supreme Court for matters at the Federal level. The original jurisdiction for crimes is at the State level where the crime is committed, with appeals that may end up at the Supreme Court after going through the lower courts.

**Article III, Section 3**  *"Treason against the United States, shall consist only in levying War against them, or in adhering to their Enemies, giving them Aid and Comfort. No Person shall be convicted of Treason unless on the Testimony of two Witnesses to the same overt Act, or on Confession in open Court.*

*The Congress shall have Power to declare the Punishment of Treason, but no Attainder of Treason shall work Corruption of Blood, or Forfeiture except during the Life of the Person attainted."*

*Corruption of Blood refers to the limit of Congressional charge and punishment of treason to the person who committed the treasonous act and not to that person's family.*

**Article IV, Section 1** **"Full Faith and Credit shall be given in each State to the public Acts, Records, and judicial Proceedings of every other State. And the Congress may by general Laws prescribe the Manner in which such Acts, Records and Proceedings shall be proved, and the Effect thereof."**

*With the three branches of the Federal government defined, framers of the Constitution continued with Article IV, which focuses on the States.*

*Section 1 states that the States need to be transparent to each other. Transparency of the States is as important as transparency of the Federal government to help prevent unneeded competition and ill will.*

**Article IV, Section 2** **"The Citizens of each State shall be entitled to all Privileges and Immunities of Citizens in the several States.**

**A Person charged in any State with Treason, Felony, or other Crime, who shall flee from Justice, and be found in another State, shall on Demand of the executive Authority of the State from which he fled, be delivered up, to be removed to the State having Jurisdiction of the Crime.**

**No Person held to Service or Labour in one State, under the Laws thereof, escaping into another, shall, in Consequence of any Law or Regulation therein, be discharged from such Service or Labour, but shall be delivered up on Claim of the Party to whom such Service or Labour may be due."**

*The first sub section in Section 2 reminds States that they need to treat citizens from another State the same as they treat citizens from their State. This is an area that the South had a lot*

153

*of trouble with during the Civil War. They did not want to treat black citizens the same as their own, even if a State from the north fully recognizes them as citizens.*

*The remaining two sub sections endure that a person cannot flee their responsibilities or obligations just by going across State lines.*

**Article IV, Section 3** *"New States may be admitted by the Congress into this Union; but no new State shall be formed or erected within the Jurisdiction of any other State; nor any State be formed by the Junction of two or more States, or Parts of States, without the Consent of the Legislatures of the States concerned as well as of the Congress.*

*The Congress shall have Power to dispose of and make all needful Rules and Regulations respecting the Territory or other Property belonging to the United States; and nothing in this Constitution shall be so construed as to Prejudice any Claims of the United States, or of any particular State."*

*Section 3 allows Congress to admit new States into the Union. It also requires State legislature and Congressional consent to subdivide or combine States into one, similar to West Virginia being created from Virginia.*

**Article IV, Section 4** *"The United States shall guarantee to every State in this Union a Republican Form of Government, and shall protect each of them against Invasion; and on Application of the Legislature, or of the Executive (when the Legislature cannot be convened), against domestic Violence."*

*Section 4 declares that States are guaranteed to have a republican form of government and the right to be protected at the Federal level.*

*The "domestic violence" clause originally was meant to cover insurrections against each other. They used the term "domestic violence" to cover acts against each other that had not been contemplated. Liberal interpretations of this clause need to weigh the gravity of the violence against the cost of its prevention, for each have a potential negative impact on the citizens of the United States or the children and grandchildren of the citizens.*

<u>Article V</u> **"The Congress, whenever two thirds of both Houses shall deem it necessary, shall propose Amendments to this Constitution, or, on the Application of the Legislatures of two thirds of the several States, shall call a Convention for proposing Amendments, which, in either Case, shall be valid to all Intents and Purposes, as Part of this Constitution, when ratified by the Legislatures of three fourths of the several States, or by Conventions in three fourths thereof, as the one or the other Mode of Ratification may be proposed by the Congress; Provided that no Amendment which may be made prior to the Year One thousand eight hundred and eight shall in any Manner affect the first and fourth Clauses in the Ninth Section of the first Article; and that no State, without its Consent, shall be deprived of its equal Suffrage in the Senate."**

*Article V provides for revisions to the Constitution. Revisions were not seen by the framers as something that should be done all the time, but be done very deliberately and have a high standard of passage. This is why a two-thirds majority of Congress is required followed by ratification by three-fourths of the States.*

<u>Article VI</u> **"All Debts contracted and Engagements entered into, before the Adoption of this Constitution, shall be as valid against the United States under this Constitution, as under the Confederation.**

*This Constitution, and the Laws of the United States which shall be made in Pursuance thereof; and all Treaties made, or which shall be made, under the Authority of the United States, shall be the supreme Law of the Land; and the Judges in every State shall be bound thereby, any Thing in the Constitution or Laws of any State to the Contrary notwithstanding.*

*The Senators and Representatives before mentioned, and the Members of the several State Legislatures, and all executive and judicial Officers, both of the United States and of the several States, shall be bound by Oath or Affirmation, to support this Constitution; but no religious Test shall ever be required as a Qualification to any Office or public Trust under the United States."*

*<u>Article VII</u> "The Ratification of the Conventions of nine States, shall be sufficient for the Establishment of this Constitution between the States so ratifying the Same."*

*The Word, "the," being interlined between the seventh and eighth Lines of the first Page, the Word "Thirty" being partly written on an Erazure in the fifteenth Line of the first Page, The Words "is tried" being interlined between the thirty second and thirty third Lines of the first Page and the Word "the" being interlined between the forty third and forty fourth Lines of the second Page."*

*I need a nap!*

Ford's pardon of Nixon may have backfired as it related to a bid for the 1976 election. Thus, Georgia Governor and peanut farmer Jimmy Carter was elected President on November 2, 1976, defeating incumbent Gerald Ford with just over half of the popular vote and just over 55% of the electoral vote. From a numbers perspective, the election was closer than the history books may reveal.

A swing of less than ten thousand total votes in Hawaii and Ohio would have given Ford the electoral votes he would have needed to win.

Another challenge to Ford's reelection was the Vice-Presidential debate. Bob Dole, Ford's running mate did not help Ford's chances during the debate. Dole made an off-handed comment about blaming Democrats for all the wars in the twentieth century, which rubbed many independent voters the wrong way. Twenty years later, Senator Dole had an opportunity to lose his own election to President Clinton.

Senator Dole is the only person to have to have been nominated by one of the two major political parties for both Vice President and President and not to ever have served in either post.

## November 3, 1976

*The corruption that plagued the Nixon administration certainly did not help Ford. That and I am not certain anyone really knew what Ford's plans were to help the country. The biggest thing that stuck in people's minds is the pardon of Dick. After the landslide in 1972, it would not have been expected for Democrats to regain control of the White House.*

*In a way, I feel sorry for Ford. He may have been a good candidate in his own right, but the tie to the Nixon presidency obviously hurt him. He may have been better off not accepting Dick's offer. I wonder if he had any clue about what was going to happen with Watergate. It was certainly simmering when he took the post.*

*The fortunate part of the process was that the Constitution worked as designed and amended and the country was once again able to peacefully make it through a transition of power.*

# Chapter 19 – 1977

On August 4, 1977, a bill creating the United States Department of Energy was signed into law by President Carter. The Department of Energy became a cabinet level agency and combined a number of programs from a variety of agencies with three agencies, the Federal Energy Administration, Energy Research and Development Administration and the Federal Power Commission. James Schlesinger became the first Secretary of Energy.

In the early 1970's, the United States was in need of a set of energy policies that protected the people from experiencing energy shortages. President Carter's short-term response of sitting next to a fire with a sweater on and telling the public to keep their thermostats at fifty-five degrees was not being received very well by the populous.

The new department also was charged with protecting the nation from becoming too reliant on a foreign supply of energy that would compromise national security.

## August 5, 1977

*I would like to see the United States figure out a way to be self-sufficient where it comes to energy. Energy is important; some argue the lifeblood of the economy. To the extent that foreign countries believe that, then it might as well be true.*

*We have enough smart people and access to resources that we should be able to become safely and efficiently energy independent and at some point, perhaps, an energy exporter.*

*National security should not be based on our need to keep our energy suppliers out of trouble. Rather, we can be more effective by continuing to lead by example and basing military decisions on issues that are more relevant rather than our gluttonous needs, particularly as perceived by the rest of the world.*

*Now that we have demonstrated our ability to beat the odds and go to the moon and back, our next challenge should be to become energy independent. Just like any other industry we focus on, I would anticipate that our scientists would be able to develop new forms of energy that we have not even dreamed of and the United States would continue to demonstrate to the world that a democratic republic is a political strategy that focuses on its citizens. A citizenry that is empowered, motivated and stretched into new horizons will accept and embrace the challenges before them and certainly and wholly succeed.*

On August 16, 1977, Elvis Presley died in Graceland. Elvis was born in Tupelo Mississippi, moved to Memphis as a teenager and died at his nearly 14-acre estate "Graceland" in Memphis.

To many, Elvis was more than just the King of Rock and Roll, he was in icon. His relative quick climb to success, ability to remake his brand and his longevity may have been contributors to his icon status. Some would attribute his icon status to his hips.

Elvis' rise to the top started in 1953 as the young singer was in the process of trying to find himself and his rhythm. He was a good ballad singer, catching the attention of Sun Record head Sam Phillips. He hooked up with Colonel Parker, who proceeded to help form the music Elvis would sing and the venues he would perform.

After a number of his hits hit number one, Elvis was drafted into the Army in 1958 and was soon shipped off to Friedberg Germany. It was in Friedberg where Elvis met the fourteen-year-old Priscilla Beaulieu, whom he married when she was twenty-one. Amphetamines, karate and Priscilla were not the only non-military activities that Elvis participated in while serving his country. He also managed to cut ten top forty hits.

In 1960, Sergeant Presley was honorably discharged from the Army and took Nashville and Memphis to Hollywood. While he did not receive an Oscar for his movie performances in Hollywood, he made a lot of money for himself, his label, and his studio. Of Elvis' thirty-three movies, twenty-seven came out in the 1960's. Also in the 60's, possibly related to the exposure from the movies, he charted to number one with seven albums and thirteen singles.

Elvis' career continued strong with some difficulties into the 1970s. Just before he was to fly out to start another tour, Elvis was found on the floor of his bathroom on August 16, 1977.

Post mortem, Elvis had two albums and six singles hit number one (including "Way Down" which came out on June 6, 1977 and was the only hit that was new, not a remix or reissue). In 1986, Elvis was in the very first class of individuals inducted into the Rock and Roll Hall of Fame.

### August 17, 1977

*Elvis Presley was one of my favorite performers. One minute, he would be singing a ballad, ripping the hearts out of his audience. The next song could be a spiritual, hearts would be heavy with how moving, and stirring his voice was. His next song could be a rock and roll number, complete with screaming teenagers, each of whom would gladly give their hearts to the King of Rock and Roll.*

*I enjoyed watching him on television, particularly his musical performances. I must admit, I was not as fond of his movies. I suppose had I been a female teenager, which I understand was the general target audience; my opinion may have been different.*

*It is unfortunate his life appeared not to be as happy as it should have been with his fame and fortune. People seem to handle fame differently. Based on what I have seen, and given my opportunity to contemplate such things, the issue for some is that when they are designated a star, the term goes to their head and they consider themselves above everything, in the stratosphere. Others who get the star designation have their feet firmly on the ground. This grounding of their life tends to make them happier with what they have accomplished and more practical in how they live their life.*

*Stars do not need to be in the sky, and are not always something for everyone to look up to. At the end of the day, they are people, with feelings and motivators like many who are not stars. Paraphrasing a famous radio broadcaster/DJ, you will always be happy if you can keep your feet on the ground while reaching for the stars.*

On September 7, 1977, there were two treaties signed by the governments of the United States and Panama, both dealing with the Panama Canal. Signatories for the two governments were President Carter on behalf of the United States and General Omar Torrijos on behalf Panama. Torrijos was the commander of Panama's National Guard. It is a bit irregular that the United States would enter a treaty agreement with someone who gained control of a country via a coup and was not democratically elected. The justification for this irregularity was that it was the understanding of the United States that the people of Panama supported Torrijos.

The Treaty Concerning the Permanent Neutrality and Operation of the Panama Canal was the first treaty signed and is relatively self-explanatory. The United States agreed to give up control of the Panama Canal with the understanding that it would remain open and apolitical. As a failsafe, the United States would continue to be the enforcer of that neutrality through military defense if needed.

The Panama Canal Treaty was signed next. This treaty gave up United States control of the Panama Canal effective on midnight on December 31, 1999 at the century ticked to 2000. It provided that Panama would operate the canal and provide for its defense.

The treaties were ratified on October 23, 1977 by Panama and the United States. The United States vote came via a Congressional consent for ratification of the first treaty on March 16, 1978 and the second on April 18, 1978.

As the century turned, besides the Panama Canal, other assets that the United States built and maintained were turned over to the Panamanians. Assets amounted to almost 400,000 square acres of land and about seven thousand buildings that included schools, residences, warehouses and a variety of other buildings.

## September 8, 1977

*I think that in general it was a good move by President Carter to turn the Panama Canal back over to the Panamanians. The United States stepped in and was the primary impetus to getting the Panama Canal built and managed. This created a vital throughway for ocean vessels saving countless time and resources from the necessity of going around South America to traverse from one ocean to the other.*

*The Panama Canal has been relatively void of political issues since the United States has been involved and the clause that the United States can step back in if there are future political issues should be a deterrent for nefarious activities.*

*The one element of concern of this transition is to whom we are transitioning. We could be giving the impression that we are condoning the fact that General Torrijos has assumed authority after a coup and not being democratically elected. This goes against the basic principles that we have strived to apply consistently for years. A precedent of dealing with unelected heads of State may make it challenging in the future for the United States credibly to apply that principle.*

# Chapter 20 – 1978

The Camp David Accords were signed by Menachem Begin, Prime Minister of Israel and Anwar Sadat, President of Egypt on September 17, 1978.

Almost as soon as the dust settled on his swearing in, President Carter saw as one of his potential legacies to secure peace in the Middle East. Carter began immediately working on attempting to attain peace by focusing on the issues between Egypt and Israel.

The term "Accords" was used rather than treaty, because the result of Camp David negotiations was two frameworks – one for short term peace and one for a longer term peace treaty.

The Framework for Peace in the Middle East was cut back from the region-wide peace that was being sought during the Ford administration. In addition to the recognition of the Palestinians and what to do with the Gaza strip and the West Bank, the original plan was to include Syria, Lebanon and the Golan Heights. It was determined that the inclusion of those areas into the framework would cause additional complexities and success may be easier to attain starting with a smaller chunk. Ultimately, the United Nations did not go along with this Framework because it did not include recognition of sovereignty for the Palestinians.

The Framework for the Conclusion of a Peace Treaty between Egypt and Israel on its face was not a lot more than an agreement to work something out. In fact, by 1978 they did work something out, which pleased the international community enough that the Norwegians and Swedes honored Begin and Sadat with the Nobel Peace Prize.

Peace was only temporary, in part because the entire region did not participate. Because of what others in the Middle East characterized as too many conciliations to the Israelis, Sadat was ostracized from the rest of the region. Sadam Hussein took advantage of this weakness and began taking over power. Three years after receiving the Nobel Peace Prize, Sadat was assassinated.

## September 18, 1978

*President Carter made great foreign policy strides with the signing of the peace accords. The people of Israel have been on the short end of the stick for centuries. Every place they end up in seems to be an issue. Moreover, it is not as if the desert regions they are fighting for are at all similar to Palm Springs. Rather, the small pieces of land that they end up inhabiting are not always prime real estate.*

*If they were not so tied to being close to their religious roots, the United States could potentially sell them some property somewhere and they would be easier to protect from the neighborhood bullies. Obviously, asking them to give up their land is not a practical solution, but perhaps in the end should be considered. The countries in the Middle East seem to be a long ways away from having the grassroots strength necessary to overthrow tyrannical control. United States intervention tends to be like putting a butterfly bandage on a wound that requires a tourniquet. Until the people can manage to put into power*

165

*someone who will strive to create a political system that is self-sustaining, outside of a tyranny, the butterflies may be all we can do.*

The Foreign Intelligence Surveillance Act (FISA) was signed into law on October 25, 1978. This Act served as public documentation of the rules that would be followed when collecting information, including Congressional oversight. Senator Ted Kennedy brought the bill to the Senate.

In addition to establishing policies and procedures for the legal collection of information designed to protect the national interest, the Act established a FISA court. The FISA court is comprised of eleven judges serving terms of seven years and appointed by the Chief Justice of the Supreme Court. The role of the FISA court is to rule on the appropriateness of foreign intelligence gathering that should be applied to the various documents, methods and artifacts brought before them.

## October 26, 1978

*It is wise that the collection of foreign intelligence information as specified by the new Foreign Intelligence Surveillance Act is to a certain degree managed by the courts. This adds appropriate checks and balances, particularly with the Congressional oversight that is also called for.*

*Even if to a large degree the court rulings that are part of this Act are for optics, the process has the appearance of propriety and a specific method of challenging intelligence collection activities even if it is after the fact.*

*Technologies for intelligence gathering have changed dramatically through the years. One only needs to watch a James Bond movie to see the potential of technology in gathering information. It is conceivable that this Act will need to be modified as technologies change. A clause that could have been added to this Act, and perhaps should be considered for similar legislation in the future is a clause that calls for a mandatory periodic review of the management of the policies and processes associated with the Act and identification of improvements given the current state of technology.*

The Humphrey-Hawkins Full Employment Act was signed into law by President Carter on October 27, 1978. House representative Augustus Hawkins and Senator Hubert Humphrey sponsored the bill.

The country was in the middle of a deep recession with high inflation and American voters were losing confidence in the Democratic Party. President Carter's potential for a second term was seemingly becoming more remote.

The bill focused on seven tenets that were deemed keys to the four major goals to get the country out of recession: full employment, increase in production, reduction of inflation, and balanced trade. The seven tenets to address these goals included; rely on private enterprise rather than the federal government, balance the budget, establish a balance in trade, modify federal reserve policies to maintain long-term growth, minimize inflation, promote price stability, and obtain Presidential leadership in setting economic goals and establishing policy to meet those goals and require the federal reserve to align monetary policy with the changes to the administrative policy.

## October 28, 1978

*The underlying policies behind the Full Employment Act are a step in the right direction and should go a long way to get the United States out of the current recession. Without a successful push in these directions, I do not see how the Democrats will come out well during the 1980 election cycle.*

*The first area, relying on private enterprise rather than government is a key to private sector growth. Government cannot spend its way out of a recession. It may have appeared to work to*

167

*get us out of the depression, but what may have gotten us out of
the depression, which does not get mentioned often, is the new set
of strong and competent workers that were created while the men
were fighting for the country - women!*

*Women entered all aspects of the workforce, from
manufacturing to small business. They showed themselves to be
hard working and just as able to produce as well as men. The
'product' that the country was able to produce was essentially
doubled. Roosevelt's government sponsored work was a catalyst
to helping make certain that the huge influx of workers would not
negatively affect employment. Ultimately, private enterprise
turned that booster shot of influx of capital and expanded in a way
that has not since been matched.*

*Replicating a similar situation today may not be as
successful. Today, there is not the massive increase in the
workforce to carry the push of government into a new wave of
expansion. Rather, government policy should be to look for ways
to get out of the way of enterprise by reducing taxes, eliminating
costly policies that get in the way of growth, and opening up
foreign trade so businesses have more opportunities to increase
demand for their goods and services. The worst thing to do is
establish policies that decrease the workforce. Obviously, it is
impossible to grow when you are shrinking.*

*The other key area in the Full Employment Act is for the
federal government to balance the budget. Ultimately, increased
debt will create a situation where growth, instead of feeding on
itself and building the economy, falls into the black hole of
servicing and paying off the debt. Overly simplified, there are two
major levers to balancing the budget - money coming in and
money going out.*

*The primary source of money coming in is through taxes.
Nevertheless, increasing taxes puts an increased burden on
workers and companies. This burden causes a contraction, not
expansion. The time to increase taxes is during an economic boom
and focusing on not spending it all, but creating a federal rainy*

*day fund that can be tapped when the economy is struggling. In a
sense, it would smooth the natural tidal flow of the economy.*

*The primary source of money going out is spending.
Seeking out areas of redundancy and waste is a first step, and can
yield some real savings. The other benefit of controlling spending
is to increase the perception of the taxpayers that the money they
are sending to Washington D.C. is being used wisely. It is harder
to convince someone to spend more when they do not think the
money is currently being used efficiently.*

*I always go back to what I was taught as a young boy -
you can have anything you want, you just cannot have everything
you want. This simple statement made me constantly weigh the
priorities and focus on the things that were highest priority.
When doing this, I was able to achieve what I wanted even though
I did not get everything.*

The Jonestown Massacre was essentially a coordinated
suicide of nine hundred and nine United States citizens. The
suicide took place at the direction of cult leader Jim Jones as he
directed his 'faithful' to drink a concoction of poison, which caused
death in less than ten minutes. Men, women, and children followed
the commands of Jones, ingested the poison and died. Jim Jones
chose a bullet to the head for his apparent suicide.

The cult-wide suicide was the ultimate result of a number of
factors that were beginning to dissect the cult-like continuity that
Jones was targeting and able to achieve for the people.
Unfortunately, the life that Jones had promised followers when
they settled in Guyana turned out to be not what he told them,
primarily because they could not farm the land as they had hoped.

Family members were constantly trying to get information
on what their family members were doing with Jones and tried to
talk them into coming home. A further complication was that Jones
was told, not too long before the suicide, that he might have lung
cancer. This information may have brought Jones' own mortality in
his mind to question. Finally, there was a delegation of family

members and others led by Congressman Leo Ryan from California who wanted to get a first-hand view of what was going on in Jonestown. As many of the delegation were leaving by plane, gunmen opened fire, killing five and injuring others.

These events triggered Jones to initiate the "White Nights" scenario where cult members went through a rehearsed process of taking the poison and dying. Some escaped, but the majority of the cult died.

## November 19, 1978

*It is amazing that someone can have enough control over so many people that a mass suicide can happen like the one in Guyana. It does not appear that the followers were drugged, but it is apparent that their souls were somehow so dedicated to the leader that encouraged the massive following of people taking their own lives. Almost one thousand people were guided to their deaths. It is difficult to penetrate a culture that is so strong to exchange one set of principles as with which the adults in the cult were likely raised, for another. Very sad.*

# Chapter 21 – 1979

On March 28, 1979, a reactor at the Three Mile Island nuclear reactor plant in Dauphin County, Pennsylvania partially melted down and released some radioactive gases and iodine gases into the surrounding environment.

A combination of mechanical failures, poorly trained workers, and an overly complicated disaster identification process led to the radioactive release.

The subsequent billion-dollar clean up lasted about fourteen years. Fortunately, follow-up studies indicated that no significant instances of radiation-caused ill effects occurred because of the release. While these studies have been questioned, there has been little evidence that the release resulted in as catastrophic consequences as originally thought it might.

### March 29, 1979

*The disaster at Three Mile Island is a reminder that safety needs to be the number one concern when dealing with something that has the potential to be a very long lasting impact to people*

171

*and the environment. It is unfortunate that this accident happened, as the United States was taking some good steps forward in becoming more energy independent. Nuclear energy can be a viable source of energy if we can learn from the mistakes made in Pennsylvania and apply them to this and the next application of nuclear technology.*

*Funding of scientists to look for more ways to keep this technology safe is a better reaction (pardon the use of the word) than a total declaration of defeat. Air travel would not be as matter of fact, as it is today if there were no lessons learned and capitalized on during the early days of flight. People today feel safer in an airplane than driving on the highways. Nuclear energy may not be the only solution to energy issues of the country, but it should not be discarded until it gets a full opportunity to demonstrate its viability.*

# Chapter 22 – 1980

On March 18, 1980, the Refugee Act was signed into law by President Carter. The Refugee Act allowed for a rapid immigration process for individuals with whom there is a humanitarian concern. "Quota" numbers of refugees were nearly tripled by this law from 17,400 50,000.

Senator Ted Kennedy began preparing a bill similar to the language in the final Act in 1978 and brought it to the Senate in 1979. The Senate voted unanimously to adopt the bill.

An important part of the Act was to help ensure refugees were smoothly assimilated into the United States culture so they had better opportunities to succeed and be self-sufficient. Per the bill, they were to receive employment training, English language instruction, cash assistance and help in finding jobs.

### March 19, 1980

*Immigration is important to the United States. After all, we are a nation of immigrants. The Refugee Act is an important piece of legislation to make certain the flow of immigration*

173

*continues.  One of the factors that sets the United States apart from the rest of the world is the extent that immigration is more free and broad.  This is partially because we have room and because it is part of our melting pot culture to be inclusive.  A country like England could be all-inclusive as far as their immigration laws are concerned, but there is a limit to their ability to expand their population because they are on an island.  The days of conquering new land around the world should be long over as most corners of Earth are already spoken for - at least the corners that someone would like to live in.*

*Immigration is similar to getting football tickets.  It is much more difficult to get tickets at Notre Dame than at Harvard.  The demand for Notre Dame tickets is higher, in part, because Notre Dame historically has a better team.  Harvard is an excellent University, but not known for its football program.*

*There are several aspects of immigration for which we need to be aware.  One of them is the number of immigrants that we want to target every year.  I did not notice that the new Act covered this the way I would have.  A simple formula should be derived that takes into account two economic factors - workforce needs and economic conditions.  While workforce needs should not exclude immigrants, it should help prioritize.  This keeps the influx in line with our needs to continue economic growth.  Of course, there should always be a percentage that is not tied to any specific need.*

*The other economic factor is the general health of the economy.  The quota, rather than being a fixed number that Congress must set subject to political pressures one way or the other, should be set based on the country's ability to absorb immigrants into our overall economy.  It is not fair to the immigrants that their opportunities are limited by a struggling economy.  Nor is it fair to current taxpayers to be burdened by potential welfare support for immigrants that do not happen to have the opportunity to be contributing members of society.*

*The assimilation component of the Refugee Act is along the lines of setting quota targets based on current economic conditions and ensuring that the opportunities exist for a smooth assimilation. The two ways that we provide opportunity for immigrants is economic opportunity to succeed and to provide immigrants with training and education to assist them in finding a job and ultimately helping them become a productive member of society.*

*As I have made clear in the past, almost twenty years ago, it is better for the collective American society for individuals to drive the opportunities that the United States offers not by relying on government to provide the specific opportunities but for people to make the opportunities for themselves. Government can be there if you stumble and fall, but you should want to get up and keep moving forward. Therefore, the collective is, together, growing opportunities and not settling for status quo – or a retreat.*

Much to the disappointment of athletes, many of who trained their entire lives, President Carter announced on March 21, 1980 that the United States would boycott the Olympic Games in Moscow because of the Soviet invasion into Afghanistan.

For many athletes, there is only one opportunity to make the Olympic team because it only happens every four years. For some events, to be competitive on the word stage, the athlete must be at a peak level of performance, which typically is affected by age. For example, there are not many older gymnasts. A young woman is typically peaking at seventeen. If her peak happens to correspond to the holding of the Olympics, she is at an advantage. If she instead must wait four more years until she is twenty-one, she may have bypassed her opportunity.

At the beginning of 1980, Jimmy Carter attempted to encourage the Soviets to withdraw their troops from Afghanistan. He gave them one month to withdraw or the United States would not participate in the Olympics the Soviets were hosting. Sanctions are not often worthwhile with the Russians and this one was no exception. After drawing the first line in the sand, the United States erased that line and drew another, which was again ignored by the Russians. They knew President Carter was relatively weak domestically and they may have been thinking that the United States was bluffing and were calling the bluff. In fact, with the United States not participating in the games, they had a much better opportunity to win the medal count and demonstrate their athletic superiority over the world, generating a great deal of country pride.

Ultimately, the United States did not compete and was joined by sixty-five other countries in the boycott. Other notable countries that joined the United States in the boycott included Canada, China, Japan, and West Germany. Other countries that did not boycott (including Australia, France, and the United Kingdom), sent their athletes to compete under the Olympic flag rather than their national flag. During medal ceremonies for these athletes, the Olympic anthem was played rather than their national anthem.

At the end of the Olympic competition in Moscow, the tradition had been to raise the flag of the next host nation. The 1984 games were to be held in Los Angeles and instead of the American flag; the Russians raised the Los Angeles flag.

## May 21, 1980

*I have been following the story of the United States participation in the Olympics in Moscow this year and very much disagree with President Carter's decision to boycott the games. I do not believe the action is to protect the athletes, but rather will result in many athletes' dreams being dashed by a political decision. Did we not learn from Vietnam regarding participation in regional conflicts? If we are worried about importing foreign oil, we should reduce or eliminate our reliance on it.*

*I do not believe that athletes should be negatively impacted and I do not believe that the action will in any way deter Russia from their political ideals and direction. The only thing they may learn is to wait until you finish hosting the Olympics before invading a country, as it does not look good. It is against what the Olympics stand for.*

*The other way to look at the situation would be to have the United States rather than boycott the games, to take the opportunity to demonstrate support against a show of aggression by focusing on an event like the Olympics, which is clearly counter to that aggression.*

President Carter ordered a military operation called Operation Eagle Claw to attempt to rescue fifty-two American hostages held at the U.S. embassy in Tehran. The operation failed. On April 24, 1980, eight military personnel (the first mission of Delta Force) were killed.

During the rescue attempt, sand was churned up from helicopter rotors and got into the engine of the helicopter, causing a chain reaction with another aircraft that resulted in an explosion, killing the eight servicemen.

Following the failed attempt to rescue the hostages, they were moved to multiple locations throughout Iran to discourage further rescue attempts.

## April 25, 1980

*I heard about the failed attempt to recover our hostages held in Iran. My heart is heavy for those that are illegally held against their will and the families that are impacted by their loved ones being unable to come home. It is difficult, maybe impossible, to negotiate with some people. Handling situations in foreign lands takes a combination of skill and art because everyone and every situation is different. I have come to realize this through my travels around Europe and my dealings with some significant foreign situation.*

*Some regimes understand and respond to negotiation, while others only understand force. Others are in the middle. The difficult job of the State Department is to establish and maintain relationships at the appropriate levels that help us be able to determine whether we need a megaphone or a stick or both. The other layer of challenges is control of public opinion. Not control by trying to trick the public into believing something is true that is not truth, but to educate the public in the realistic aspects of the situation. This is of course easier said than done and easier for an armchair quarterback (literally).*

*Both sides of the aisle need to be able to set aside political agendas and voices of fringe constituency and help communicate the reality of the situation. The debate can be healthy and the agenda of the State Department can be drawn into question, but at the end of the day, there quickly needs to be a common direction that everyone can agree with. Congressional action around national defense should always be clean of any other political issues or agendas that muddy the waters. Direction for foreign policy should also be high on the list of items that are debated by either the Senate or House. This provides the President with both support and cover as actions are taken.*

The cabinet level Department of Health and Human Services was officially established on May 4, 1980. As of one year prior to the establishment of this cabinet post, it was called the Department of Health, Education and Welfare. The "Education" portion was removed when the Department of Education was established in 1979.

Historically, provision for the health and welfare of the United States is not only part of the Constitution, but has been evolving since President John Adams created the Marine Hospital Service in 1798. The name established in 1798 remained until 1912, when it was changed to the Public Health Service. The scope of the department continued to increase. In 1953, after a couple other name changes, it became the Department of Health, Education and Welfare.

## May 5, 1980

*It makes sense that the Department of Education was extracted from the original Department of Health, Education and Welfare. One of the constitutional directives of the federal government is to provide opportunity by eliminating the barriers of Health and Welfare challenges that the public may face. This will continue to be an aspect in which both sides of the aisle should continue to agree until there is a deviation from the goal, so a focus on Health and Welfare is appropriate.*

*One such deviation may be a deviation from the focus of provisions for health and welfare go from an inoculation of support to prevent or eliminate the virus that is causing a citizen not to be a contributing member of society, to just enough medication to reduce the symptoms but the virus remains. We do not want to find ourselves in a position that we are only focused on the symptoms for a citizen not contributing to society rather than eradicating the virus.*

*Not eradicating the initial virus of despair can result in it migrating into a disease. A disease of settling for something less than a person's full potential. If this disease of settling, pessimism, and complacency spreads too far, then all of society suffers. Half of the population could be working to support the other half.*

*This erosion of the culture on which this country was founded must be avoided. Every lawmaker, whether more conservative or more liberal, should be able to recognize signs of pockets of the virus spreading to a nationwide disease. These recognitions need to be addressed before such time that a simple inoculation may be no longer able to affect a recovery.*

Leading in to the 1980 elections, President Carter's chances seemed bleak. The economy was barely limping along. In fact, a new word was coined to describe the county's situation – stagflation. Economic indicators of expansion of gross domestic product were being replaced by the "Misery Index".

Foreign policy was about as bleak as domestic policies with interactions with Ayatollah Khomeini as stagnant as the economy. People were lining up for gas and President Carter's approval rating fell below 30%.

Ted Kennedy, with the support of his family and an overwhelming vote of confidence coming from pollsters, decided to run against the incumbent president. Some polls had Kennedy leading Carter two to one. After much consideration, Kennedy announced his bid for the presidency on November 7, 1979, which was a year before the election.

Kennedy's campaign sputtered somewhat and, among other issues, was challenged by overcoming the Chappaquiddick incident. Challenges with the current presidency kept Kennedy's encouragement high as he took his challenge all the way to the Democratic convention. During the convention, a brutal bantering back and forth occurred reflecting the frustration with President Carter's four years.

Finally, on the final day of the convention, on August 14, 1980, Kennedy withdrew his bid for the nomination and President Carter became the nominee.

## August 14, 1980

*I see Teddy withdrew from the running for the Democratic nomination. It is difficult to run against an incumbent, but this may have been the year where a new face would have been welcome. I read that many Democrats feel that unless someone else replaces President Carter that the Republicans will win no matter who they have on their ticket.*

*Teddy was given a hard time by the press with the Chappaquiddick incident. While they overlook it in Massachusetts, the people across the country lack the connection to Teddy to do the same. I think Teddy may have finally come to the realization that, unless he can demonstrate his leadership abilities as a Governor or Vice President, that his dreams of becoming President will not amount to more than just that.*

On November 4, 1980, Ronald Reagan was elected to his first term as President of the United States, beating out incumbent President Jimmy Carter. Reagan took somewhat of a high road during the campaign and focused on the need to be more optimistic about the future of the United States. Carter, on the other hand, focused on messages that are more negative and tried to affix a right-winger label on Reagan.

Reagan had an additional burden of a fending off and splitting votes with a strong third-party candidate in John Anderson, a member of the House of Representatives from Illinois. Representative Anderson ran against Reagan in the Republican primaries and decided to make a bid as an independent candidate. Ultimately, Anderson had little impact on the Electoral College results, but was able to garner close to six million popular votes.

When the dust settled, Reagan was almost ten percentage points ahead of Carter in the popular vote and won the Electoral College by a 489 to 49 margin. Additionally, Reagan's coat tails were broad enough to allow his party to gain control of the Senate for the first time in twenty-eight years.

## November 5, 1980

*If the election of Ronald Reagan results in getting the country out of the economic doldrums where we find ourselves, then it does not matter what side of the aisle the underlying political values reside. A strong economy should be the goal of Democrats and Republicans. It is economic strength that provides opportunity for strength in all other areas and makes leadership, foreign and domestic, much easier.*

*In some respects, many of the speeches that I heard Reagan give aligned more with my views than President Carter. I spent some time thinking about why that was my impression, and decided that perhaps there are two major facets that caused my 'shift'. The first is that many of Reagan's policies aligned with directions that I might have gone if in a similar situation, particularly his feeling that Americans are too highly taxed and that tax reductions tend to be an economic stimulus.*

*The other area that resonated with me was Reagan's positive approach toward the country. We have been living in a bad stretch where we have seen long lines getting rationed gasoline and the President with his sweater on sitting by a fire in the fireplace telling Americans to turn down their thermostats to fifty-five degrees. The malaise, as some have called it, is best met with a leader that can put a positive spin on the future and show the people that there is a light at the end of the tunnel. Besides, people here in Southern California cannot even come close to relating to a fifty-five thermostat setting. I believe that if the temperature here fluctuates out of a small band of seventy-two to eighty-two, there is general unrest.*

A gunshot on December 8, 1980 meant that the Beatles would never sing together again. Mark David Chapman shot and killed John Lennon outside his apartment in New York City.

Lennon was with his wife Yoko Ono. They were arriving home from a mixing session at a music studio, when Chapman, who a few hours earlier got Lennon's autograph on a copy of Lennon's Double Fantasy album, shot him from behind.

Lennon was pronounced dead at the Roosevelt hospital from massive blood loss because of the shooting. As the doctor was making the pronunciation, the hospital PA that was playing background music, as if rehearsed, played the Beatles hit "All My Loving".

## December 9, 1980

*Who in the country is not at all touched by the senseless shooting of John Lennon last night? Besides hundreds of thousands of teenage girls that have had their collective fingers crossed for another tour of their beloved Beatles, many more followers of Rock and Roll respect what the Beatles did for this musical genre. Perhaps all the talk about Yoko Ono's impact of whether or not the band will or should be together will now be put to rest as Mr. Lennon will be.*

*At first, I was a little reluctant to embrace Rock and Roll music. My father once said that your musical taste is established when you are thirteen. Rock and Roll is very different from Guy Lombardo and the jazz music of the early 1930's. Blues music was becoming somewhat popular, but had not found its way to New England.*

# Chapter 23 – 1981

After being in captivity for four hundred and forty-four days, the fifty-two United States hostages held in Tehran were released. As if a message of contempt for President Carter, or fear of Reagan, the release occurred on January 20, 1981 immediately after President Reagan was sworn in as President and completed his inaugural address to the nation and world.

## January 21, 1981

*President Reagan got a big boost to his potential impact on the United States' foreign policy with the release of the fifty-two hostages yesterday. I am certain it was no coincidence that the release was so well orchestrated with Reagan's inaugural speech. There are many family members that will be glad when their loved ones finally set foot back on American soil.*

On April 12, 1981 Columbia, the name of the first United States Space Shuttle, was launched and began orbiting the Earth. After a six-year United States hiatus from launching a person into orbit, Columbia's maiden voyage began a series of missions. The most important mission was to prove that an aircraft could be designed to return through the Earth's atmosphere in condition to be able to be launched again later. This design was an attempt to create a repeatable process rather than the use-once spacecraft that had been designed to date.

The shuttle spacecraft still relied on significantly sized booster rockets to launch it into orbit. Rather than the craft sitting on top of the rockets designed to lift it into space, the shuttle was strapped onto the side of the rockets.

Columbia's short mission, which only lasted just over two days, was mainly to test out the ability to launch and safely land the spacecraft. Another unique aspect of Columbia was that it landed similar to a plane, but more like a glider. It did not have a propulsion system like propellers or jet engines to give it the ability to be flown. Rather, once getting through the Earth's atmosphere, it acted like a controlled glider – one that weighed a hundred tons. Columbia landed at Edwards Air Force Base in California and was returned to Florida atop a converted aircraft designed to transport a large aircraft, a modified Boeing 747.

## April 20, 1981

*I am pleased that the United States has found a way to continue space exploration. From the time of the early explorers, inhabitants of the world have always had a desire not to be satisfied with the status quo. One of the ways they have stretched themselves is through exploration. Now that we know the Earth is round and have charted all of the large landmasses and most of the small ones, exploration can take two directions. One direction is to the oceans. With two-thirds of the Earth being covered by water, there is likely a lot under the water that we do not know. Frankly, I would be satisfied simply to sail the oceans, but I am certain there are many who spend their lives exploring and understanding the ecosystems beneath the beauty of the waves on top.*

*The other direction is, reaching toward the stars. Today, we are somewhat limited by technology as to how far we can seek out past our protective atmosphere. However, based on some television shows I have seen, there are many people with imaginations about possible space travel. Imagination results in the expansion of what we know to new inventions and discoveries.*

*The technology that has been invented that allows the Shuttle to leave our atmosphere and go into space, orbit Earth, and essentially fly back into the atmosphere and land like an airplane is incredible. I wonder how many young children in junior high school have sketched spacecraft that closely resembled the Space Shuttle. Some of those children are likely scientists working on the shuttle project today. They could be engineers, architects, or astronauts.*

*Government's investment in helping these people realize their dreams keeps us expanding our horizons, reaching for the stars and giving today's youth something to dream about so the cycle can continue in perpetuity.*

On August 13, 1981, President Reagan signed the Economic Recovery Tax Act into law. This legislation was also called the Kemp-Roth Tax Cut, named after the congressional Representatives that brought the bill to the floor, Representative Jack Kemp and Senator William Roth.

This bill was subject of a series of debates in the House and Senate with the primary area of focus being the amount of tax cuts that would be on the final version. Both sides were somewhat disappointed because the final amount was not big enough for one side of the debate or small enough for the other. As the final bill reflected, the highest tax rate was reduced from seventy percent to fifty percent. The lowest rate was reduced from fourteen percent to eleven percent. The cuts also reduced corporate tax rates and estate taxes among other areas that affected revenues.

The short-term effect was, as most expected a decrease in federal government revenue. This revenue reduction resulted in an increase in the deficit to $221 billion dollars after the first four years of the reduction of taxes. Then, in the next three years as the stimulus took effect, the economy gained momentum and revenues quickly rose and the deficit was reduced to $152 billion.

## August 14, 1981

*I found the text of a speech I made to the New York Economic Club on December 14, 1962. "This administration pledged itself last summer to an across-the-board, top-to-bottom cut in personal and corporate income taxes to be enacted and become effective in 1963. I am not talking about a quickie or a temporary tax cut, which would be more appropriate if a recession were imminent. Nor am I talking about giving the economy a mere shot in the arm to ease some temporary complaint. The federal government's most useful role is not to rush into a program of excessive increases in public expenditures, but to expand the incentives and opportunities of private expenditures.*

*When consumers purchase more goods, plants use more of their capacity, men are hired instead of laid off, investment increases, and profits are high. Corporate tax rates must also be cut to increase incentives and the availability of investment capital. The government has already taken major steps this year to reduce business tax liability and to stimulate the modernization of our productive plant and equipment."*

*President Reagan's views on reducing taxes to stimulate the economy still make sense twenty years later. Incentives for consumers to spend, businesses to invest and governments to control growth are keys to economic recovery and prosperity.*

# September 1, 1981

*Well, there is one time of the year that I get confused and hopefully not because I am getting old. The last four months in the year: September, October, November, and December all have Latin roots in their names. They are the Latin roots for the numbers: seven, eight, nine and ten, respectively. The seventh month should be September and the tenth month December. However, thanks to Caesar, two months were inserted after June, pushing the last four months out to the end. So now, the numerical representation of October is "10" and not "8". I hope Julius (July) and Augustus (August) are happy.*

# Chapter 24 – 1982

An estimated one million people crowded into New York City's Central Park to protest the nuclear arms race on June 12, 1982. This was the largest demonstration of its kind as of 1982, but was just one of many protests against both the nuclear proliferation associated with the Cold War with Russia and the use of nuclear fuel to generate energy.

### June 13, 1982

*It is likely daunting to the youth of America to think that another country has a nuclear arsenal big enough to annihilate the entire United States. Moreover, on the other side of the world, there are Russian youth thinking the same thing about the United States.*

*The build-up of nuclear arsenals on either side of the world was done so as a deterrent so the other side will not use their weapons. To the youth that are demonstrating for peace it is not much more than two neighbors building fences higher and higher, two feet apart to keep the other neighbor from stealing his*

189

*chickens. At some level, it seems unnecessary because both neighbors already have chickens. The issue is that they live in fear that the other guy will steal his chickens and he will not have them anymore. The protesters, who are across the street watching the two men building higher and higher fences are wondering why they cannot simply agree to raise their own chickens and either eat them or collect their eggs, but not be swayed by what the other guy is doing. All the while, the onlookers are wondering about the efficiency of two identical fences two feet apart.*

*World leaders need to determine how to tear down the fences and discuss issues rationally without needing the threat of mutual annihilation.*

# Chapter 25 – 1983

President Reagan proposed the Strategic Defense Initiative on March 23, 1983.  The goal of the Strategic Defense Initiative was to leverage NASA technologies using satellite systems coupled with ground-based technologies to protect the United States from nuclear ballistic missiles.

Reagan was not a proponent of building up nuclear arsenals to match the arsenals of Russia and rely on a possibility of Mutual Assured Destruction to allay the possibilities of initiation of nuclear warfare.  Rather, a protection system that may result in less damage in the United States than on Russia if both sides fired all their intercontinental missiles at once.

Many questioned the viability of a system that was able to intercept and destroy missiles before they are able to hit their targets, but Reagan continued to profess that not only was it possible, but that the United States was well under way in perfecting the technology.

Russia was spending all of its time creating more nuclear missiles, enough to obliterate the entire world several times over.

Whether or not if it was a bluff, the action that President Reagan took pushed the United States ahead of Russia and provided opportunities for future negotiations.

## March 24, 1983

*President Reagan's focus on using technology for enhancing the defense of the country is excellent. We may be able to save lives of our young men who defend us so bravely.*

*I believe my sentiments when I was President were similar to Reagan's actions that money should not be the limiting factor when our national defense is at stake. Gambling with our money is certainly not as risky as gambling with our lives.*

## August 12, 1983

*I remember one summer when I was young and we were spending a lot of time playing various games outside. It seemed like we were always getting in trouble for bringing things inside, that we were told belonged outside. I'm not certain how it happened, but I seemed to collect mostly rocks in my pockets, but sometimes other things like coins, bugs, pieces of my brother's clothing, and other odds and ends.*

*One day, there appeared a wooden box strategically placed inside the back door, which is the one we were told to use. When we asked what the box was for, we were told that every time we came inside that we needed to empty our pockets into the box. At first, we sporadically remembered the pocket discharge task, but after a few stern reminders, and one a bit more than stern, we remembered.*

*The box began filling up. The clutter from our day's exploits. One day, I caught a frog in the back yard in the middle of a running game; I believe it was a variant of tag. Therefore, of course, into the pocket he went. He was small, so it did not seem as though there was anything there. In addition, in retrospective, it is a good thing I did not fall down and have a squished frog in my pocket.*

*Soon, we were called to prepare for dinner. I emptied my pockets into the box and as could be expected, the frog plopped into the box with the other treasures. I did not have time to find another home for the frog as we were in a hurry to get ready for dinner and I ran to the sink to wash up.*

*Later that evening, I remembered about the small frog in the box and went to the back door to retrieve it. The frog was gone. After about thirty minutes of frantic searching, the frog was nowhere to be found and I was forced to explain the situation. Now, the entire family was searching for my frog. Finally, Bobby found the hopper and was told to escort it to through back door to its freedom.*

*After that night, the box was put outside and I cannot remember doing much more pocket collecting.*

# Chapter 26 – 1984

Likely a combination of revenge for the United States boycott of the 1980 Olympics in Russia and a statement around the Cold War, most of the Eastern Bloc of nations boycotted the 1984 Olympic in Los Angeles. The intention to boycott was initially announced by the Soviet Union, who was soon joined by neighboring Hungary, Czechoslovakia, and East Germany, United States neighbor Cuba and thirteen others

### May 8, 1984

*Tit for tat. If you do not come to my Olympics, I will not come to yours. Such a silly 'Cold War' battle. The only people that suffer are the athletes - most of which likely do not even closely follow the actions that result in their inability to compete.*

### October 21, 1984

*I do not believe that there is enough focus on education during the campaigning I have heard and read this political*

*season. While the United States is gifted with abundant natural
resources, the biggest gift to which we have been endowed is our
gift to think and use our minds to benefit humanity.*

*To keep it simple, there are two prongs to any attempt to
enhance the asset of our minds – opportunity and freedom.*

*We must make certain that barriers to individuals
attaining an education are removed. One of the most discussed
barriers is the financial barrier. This is the easiest to manage,
because we only collectively need to engage in making certain
education is affordable to all, no matter what their financial
situation is. More difficult may be to make education as efficient
as possible, reducing overall costs and influencing affordability.*

*Once funding the education is overcome, the barriers are
not limited to the 'push' of children into school. The most
challenging barrier is "pulling" them there. Young minds need to
be encouraged to want to learn, which builds the basis for lifelong
learning. They need to understand the benefits of learning;
getting the job that they want, being able to sift through the
mounds of information they are bombarded with and determine for
themselves the difference between fact and fiction. They need to be
positioned to create their own opportunities.*

*Good, entry-level job opportunities need to be available
and required skills not limited to candidates with experience.
Young adults need to understand that they cannot start as
president of a company, just as it is not advisable to start as
President of the United States. Focusing on success stories about
those fortunate enough to make a quick rise is counterproductive
as it is not the norm. There are many more examples of hard
working people being successful because of their hard work, not
because they found a sack of money on the sidewalk.*

*Anything that gets in the way of young adults feeling they
can be and should be positive contributors to society, including
government policy, needs to be limited or eliminated. If not, if the
strings of government create marionettes, we are not allowing
youth to control their futures and manage their destinies.*

*Part of the pull of opportunity is assuring that youth will have freedom to pursue their dreams. There is no worse de-motivator than not being able to visualize a future that aligns with your dreams. Barriers to the freedom to achieve dreams come in a variety of flavors, and can be as individual as the dreams themselves.*

*If a young adult is provided with all of the comforts of home and is not adequately weaned from those comforts, a barrier could be the lack of determining what comforts are important and how to achieve them. If a nice house is a comfort of home and the young adult does not have any idea of what it takes to buy or rent a nice place to live, the idea of moving away from home could become insurmountable. If parents continue to support the young adult with a home or, worse yet, government decides to interfere and determine how to make the move easier; the young adult is not learning self-sufficiency.*

*On the obverse, if government expands assistance to a point where the initial goal of providing short-term help to overcome a barrier along the way turns into reliance, then there is a possibility that reliance turns into an addiction that becomes difficult resolve. The solution to the original barrier becomes a bigger barrier.*

*The other way that government can stand in the way of freedom to achieve a dream is by creating too may regulations. Regulations and rules can seem daunting to someone who is looking to start a new business or has an idea for a new product or service and working to generate demand for that product or service.*

*If there are too many rules, the game becomes too complicated to play and creativity becomes stifled under the weight of the rules. If there are so many rules that a linebacker can no longer figure out how to tackle a running back without a flag being thrown, the National Football League may become the National Flag-football League.*

# Chapter 27 – 1985

In London and Philadelphia, headliners such as Adam Ant, Elvis Costello, Sting, U2, Queen, Elton John, Paul McCartney, Joan Baez, REO Speedwagon, The Beach Boys, and Duran Duran performed a live concert to raise awareness of the famine inflicting Ethiopia.

The event was a coordinated, satellite enhanced mega concert that hoped to feature a duet between David Bowie and Mick Jagger, one in London and the other in Philadelphia. Unfortunately, the technology did not quite synch up and the simultaneous duet did not come off.

Phil Collins took advantage of the speedy Concorde jet and was able to perform at both venues.

Overall, the event is said to have brought in £150 million for relief to the people of Ethiopia and deemed a success.

### July 14, 1985

*I think it is excellent when musicians, or anyone else that is in a position to influence others, are involved in a humanitarian effort like the Live Aid concert to shine a spotlight on the famine in Ethiopia. It is incumbent on the entire world to respond to needs for food, water, basic housing, and basic medical treatment. The United States always seems to lead the way. It is to the betterment of the Earth if everyone works together so see to the basic needs of their fellow humans. Government subsidies are not always the answer, but instead can create a culture of letting someone else handle it.*

*What other countries do not seem to understand is the inherent power in doing things for others rather than only for you. There is a limit to the isolationism that can be impressed upon your people with the continued expansion of travel and technology.*

*It is somewhat embarrassing that the arena in which the musicians played in Philadelphia was named after me.*

# Chapter 28 – 1986

January 15th marks the birthday of Martin Luther King, and the first federal observance of that event was on January 20, 1986. The federal holiday was designated to be held on the third Monday in January to ensure it did not fall on a weekend and people who observed the holiday would have a three-day weekend.

President Reagan signed the bill that established the holiday in 1983 and three years later, it was an officially observed federal holiday. It was not for another fourteen years that the observance was finally passed by the final State legislature and observed at both the federal level and by all fifty states.

## January 20, 1986

*The creation of a day to remember the life and accomplishments of Dr. Martin Luther King, Jr. is a positive attestation to the firm conviction of the United States to identify an injustice like the treatment of blacks and fixing it. Just like any culture that is pervasive in a society, cultural change is difficult.*

199

*Dr. King was not only a role model for the cultural change, but unlike historical change agents, was driven to do so peacefully.*

*He knew that the likelihood of reaction to his efforts of achieving equality between whites and blacks might lead to violence on both sides. He also seemed to recognize that violence only serves to redirect attention from the message to the violence. Putting a picture of a riot on the front page of a newspaper sells more papers than the equality messages that led to the riot. Nevertheless, he saw the real strength is the power of leading with a handshake instead of a fist.*

*I have seen many schools, streets and other landmarks being named after Dr. King. I hope that those landmarks and this new federal holiday will serve to remind everyone of the message that Dr. King was sending and the method by which he chose to send it.*

Seventy-three seconds after taking off from the Kennedy Space Center, The rocket carrying the Space Shuttle Challenger exploded killing the seven-astronaut crew, including schoolteacher Christa McAuliffe.

The disaster, which grabbed the attention of the world, led to a hiatus of almost three years of manned shuttle launches while the causes of the explosion were researched and addressed.

The cause of the explosion was generally attributed to flaws in the O-rings that were designed to keep pressurized gas from escaping and interacting with components outside the fuel tank. This flaw, that was known and not addressed by the shuttle's engineers, was further exasperated by the unseasonably cold temperatures in Florida that day. Prior to the launch, manufacturers of the O-rings suggested to shuttle engineers that the launch should be delayed for warmer temperatures.

## January 28, 1986

*I was watching the shuttle mission with a great deal of interest, along with schoolchildren across the country. Then I shared their horror to watch the crew, including Christa McAuliffe, perish as the rocket and shuttle exploded just after takeoff. Their fate was certain as soon as the explosion occurred. I know the precautions are extensive that are taken to protect the astronauts who volunteer for these missions. If anything could have been done to protect this tragedy from happening, it would have.*

*In addition to the six-crew members, I feel for the family of the schoolteacher who took a hiatus from her normal classroom activities and joined the mission. I am sure they were able to share her excitement about the idea of being in space and setting an example for schoolchildren across the country to emphasize the focus on science. I hope NASA does not forget about any future attempt to include a layperson as part of the crew, although this will likely be a major setback.*

On May 19, 1986, the Firearm Owner's Protection Act was enacted that modified a number of the provisions in the Gun Control Act, which was signed into law almost twenty years earlier. The bill was initiated because of many challenges to the way the 1968 Gun Control Act had been implemented.

Research indicated that a high percentage of prosecutions under the auspices of the Gun Control Act were out of compliance from the second amendment of the constitution. This was the impetus to the determination that modifications needed to be made to clarify the original bill.

## May 20, 1986

*I have been reading that the Gun Control Act that Lyndon signed into law had some flaws in the way arrests have been made.*

*I believe in the right of American's to protect them as long as it does not impinge on the rights of others. Just like you have the freedom of speech to say what you want, you cannot yell "Fire" in a crowded movie theater and expect that the Constitution will protect you from prosecution.*

Ken Kragen conceived of a concept to help raise money for African relief – a sea to shining sea human chain. The goal was to create a human chain from Manhattan's Battery Park in New York City to the HMS Queen Mary in Long Beach California.

On Sunday May 25, 1986 for a staged period of fifteen minutes between six and seven million people held hands along the route connecting the Atlantic and Pacific oceans. The event was called Hands Across America.

There were breaks in the line in the unpopulated stretches across the country, but also places in the more populated areas where there were more than a single file line. In fact, in highly populated areas the line was up to ten people deep. Given the estimated number of people who participated, if a contiguous line could have been formed from point to point, the line would have stretched the width of the United States. The event raised over thirty million dollars.

## May 26, 1986

*While we were not part of the official chain, I had Frank and the others join me in participating in the Hands Across America human chain that connected the east and west coasts. I like these kinds of events as they cause the public to participate.*

*Participation is ultimately a stronger way to solicit and maintain support for a cause than armchair quarterbacking. It also makes people feel as if they have some power in setting or driving the course, which they do.*

Senator Barry Goldwater and Representative William Nichols combined in sponsoring the Goldwater-Nichols Act. This legislation was focused on applying reorganization to the United States Department of Defense. The bill was signed into law on October 1, 1986 after a unanimous vote in the Senate and a very high percentage of yeas in the House.

The bill reorganized the United States Department of Defense by downgrading the power of the members of the Joint Chiefs of Staff to more of an advisory role, while giving more authority to Chairman of the Joint Chiefs.

Ultimately, President Reagan wanted to provide an environment for the variety of military services to work together better. The reorganization was focused more on being able to respond to challenges around the world rather than silos of strength. The goal was to give the military more of a geographic look and feel.

Other areas of focus included procurement, which was changed to target opportunities to save budget by working with the other branches to simplify the procurement, process and save budgets by working together.

## October 2, 1986

*I understand how the various branches of service in the military get misaligned. From your first day with whichever branch you start with, you are indoctrinated into the culture of that branch. Almost by definition, you are focused on the premise that your branch is the best and you should be proud to be a part of the best. That indoctrination is important so everyone has a common mindset.*

*As you move up the ranks, the culture is carried forward. Therefore, whether on the golf course, the mess hall, or planning joint operations, there is always a bit of one-up-man-ship.*

*The other benefit that the reorganization has is the regional focus. Conducting a mission in the Pacific Ocean is very different from a mission in the Sahara desert of Africa. Having experts in each of the areas not only help each branch be better prepared, but help identify the skills that each branch can bring to bear on the situation.*

*Getting the Joint Chiefs of Staff to work together is an entirely different issue!*

President Reagan signed the Tax Reform Act of 1986 into law on October 22, 1986. This revenue neutral bill was aimed at simplifying the ever changing and burdensome tax code. Essentially, the bill was a tax cut, cutting the highest tax rate from 50% to 28% and the lowest rate was raised from 11% to 15%.

As the top rate was lowered, some loopholes and tax shelters were eliminated which attempted to maintain a relative wash in tax burden, but simplifying the calculations.

## October 23, 1986

*The yo-yo motion of taxation, where one political group increases and the next political group cuts is an interesting dynamic. If the prior administration cut taxes (in a sense, eliminating prior tax increases), you can take credit for extending the cuts and touting the savings to middle class families as if you reduced the tax yourselves.*

*The middle class is a large block of voters, bigger if the range is considered to be from poverty to 20 times poverty. Therefore, to counteract the possibility of losing that large block of voters and satiate the need for more revenue, it is necessary to choose a different group of citizens on which to impose increase taxes. You cannot choose the poor because they do not pay a high percentage of taxes, if any, and you would not be able to get much from them. The choice then, is to increase taxes for rich people. However, since the term tax increase is somewhat negative, the spin that is necessary is to call it the elimination of a cut (which*

*was the elimination of an increase, which was the elimination of a*
*cut.) Is the yo-yo metaphor becoming clearer?*

In an attempt to encourage the Lebanese to release seven
United States hostages and allow the funding of Nicaraguan
Contras, the senior executive branch officials under President
Reagan facilitated arms sales to Iran. This covert operation ran
opposite of the arms embargo against Iran. The operation was
initially uncovered and published by the Lebanese magazine Ash-
Shiraa.

The foreign operations that the United States were involved
in were related by the fact that in order for the administration
officials to be able to help fund the Contra effort to unseat the
Nicaraguan dictatorship it meant raising capital under the radar.
The best thing of value they had available was arms. Therefore,
they found a buyer for arms in Iran who was in need of arms
because of the embargo.

The transfer of the weapons was done through Israel as the
intermediary of the weapon shipment with the understanding that
the United States would replenish their weapon stores.

It was generally understood that Reagan knew about the
goal to both support the Contras' effort to eliminate the dictatorship
and operations to attempt to free the hostages. It is unclear that the
President knew the precise operations that were underway or the
linkages between the two.

Over a dozen indictments were lodged against participants
in the Iran-Contra affair. Of thirteen indictments, six were given
pardons by George H. W. Bush – Elliott Abrams, Duane Claridge,
Alan Fiers, Clair George, Robert McFarlane, and Casper
Weinberger. Three were given immunity to prosecution in
exchange for testimony – Fawn Hall, Oliver North and Jonathan
Royster. William Casey fell ill prior to his testimony. John
Poindexter's conviction was overturned by the Supreme Court.
Richard Secord pleaded guilty to making false statements to
Congress and received two years of probation. Albert Hakim plead

guilty to stealing government property, received two years of probation, and paid a $5,000 fine.

## November 4, 1986

*Helping the Nicaragua Contras defeat the dictatorial leadership seems to be a good mission. However, as I look back to the times in history where we have chosen sides in a local political struggle, we do not seem to have a good track record of choosing the right sides. On the other hand, if we do not choose sides, we may create alienation with a certain percentage of the population of the country we are trying to help.*

*Assisting countries with force may not be the best way to help, as we likely cannot police the entire world. We can offer, though, support and leadership through example. Sometimes, communication and knowledge is more powerful that arms.*

*It may not happen as quickly as we would like, but in many cases, oppressive power by the few is ultimately overcome by the many.*

# Chapter 29 – 1987

On June 12, 1987 during a visit to Berlin, President Reagan delivered a simple challenge to Soviet Premier Gorbachev reflecting on the wall that separated East and West Berlin to "tear down this wall". Leading up to Reagan's challenge, Gorbachev had been offering some vestiges of reconciliation by communicating messages of restructuring and transparency. President Reagan capitalized on the Premier's words perestroika and glasnost, which mean restructuring and transparency. These two themes were not often heard from the communist nation.

What better place to set the challenge, but in front of the divisive wall. The destruction of the wall could put Soviet action behind the words and could result in the restructuring and transparency that was envisioned by the perestroika and glasnost messages.

Kennedy's trip to the wall in 1963, over thirty years earlier, was focused on establishing the United States support of the West Berlin people and the power of democracy and people who participated in a Democratic government.

Ultimately, two and a half years after Reagan's challenge, East Berlin opened the Brandenburg gate and Germans were once again allowed unfettered access from one side of Berlin to the other.

## June 12, 1987

*I need to teach Ronnie some German.*

*Kudos to President Reagan for standing up to the Soviets and challenging the Berlin Wall as a symbol of the division between the two political philosophies.*

*It is interesting to consider the purpose of the wall in the first place. Rhetorically speaking, is it there to keep non-Communists from wanting to join the other Communists in East Berlin? On the other hand, is the wall to keep the East Berliners from sampling the flavors of Democracy?*

*Either way, it is an interference with the opportunity of the German people to choose.*

*More somewhat rhetorical questions – is it the responsibility of the United States to force the opportunity to choose? Alternatively, possibly worse, to force a choice? Who is to say that the American way is the best way? Can we not lead by example, rather than leading by force? Are we afraid that people will be satisfied with the mediocrity of socialism and not continuously want to better themselves? What is propaganda and how much control does a government have over the message if there are increasingly more ways to distribute the message?*

*The ultimate solution may be in the people themselves. Do they resolve to make themselves personally better and strive to achieve leadership that aligns with that goal? If so, will the government allow the people to self-direct what their leadership does?*

*Democracy allows for the self-direction of the people to insist by the power of the ballot that the people in government who represent them are acting with a goal that closely mimics the goals of the voters. If Democracy is scuttled and government finds a way to take the power away from the people, it could take generations to recover.*

*Fortunately, the United States has a constitution and separation of powers amongst all three branches of government to help ensure that the middle class of the country is not diminished to a point where there are those that live off the government and others that become the government.*

On Monday, October 19, 1987 millions of investors saw their retirement plans elongate as stock markets around the world crashed. In the United States, the Dow Jones Industrial Average plummeted over twenty-two percent, which was over 500 points. Stock Market aficionados refer to October 19th as Black Monday.

While many economists at the time were predicting gloom and doom for years, the most likely cause of the crash was too quick of a run up through the year up until October. There was an increase of over forty percent through the first nine plus months of the year. As more people jumped into the excited run, the market was running on emotion rather than strong financial numbers of the companies that were benefiting from the capital influx. For investors that rode the wave up from the beginning, the crash was not much more than a "should have been anticipated" correction. For others that jumped in to the market toward the end, the correction resulted in large losses.

The aggression in the Mid-East by Iran was seen as the trigger that caused jitters in the market's emotions. On October 15, 1987, Iran fired a missile at and hit an American flagged oil supertanker. On October 16, the following day, Iran hit another US ship with a missile. This aggression along with some jitters of a twelve percent drop over the previous three days led to emotions a program trading cause a chain reaction retreat of the overcapitalization of the market.

## October 20, 1987

*The Stock Market is a very good tool for Americans to invest in the future of American companies. Putting capital into corporate operations is a fundamental method that more often results in a better company and accumulation of wealth for the investors.*

*The challenge that government has in dealing with this process is to know when to step in and when to stay out of the way. Unfortunately, government has a hard time staying out of the way, as it is much easier to get involved than to get uninvolved.*

*When the federal government steps in and artificially helps, the influx of backing may result in an initial upturn in the market. Then, the question is where do you stop the help and when. An artificial boost means the market is artificially high and when the boost ends, there is one direction that it is likely to go – you only hope that it does not correct itself to a point lower than when you started.*

*The best way for government to help is to make the environment as conducive for investing as possible through fewer regulations, controlled taxation, and fair trade.*

# Chapter 30 – 1988

On August 10, 1988, President Regan signed a bill that granted reparations to those who had been interned by the United States Government during World War II.

The internship was a reaction by the Government to an executive order signed by Franklin Roosevelt to the Japanese attack on Pearl Harbor. Some still maintain that the internship was not only a way to protect the United States from domestic threats related to the war, but also to protect Japanese-Americans from possible discriminatory retribution based on their heritage.

The Civil Liberties Act was passed by the House by a 243-141 margin and by the Senate by a 69-27 margin.

The bill provided for payments totaling $20,000 for surviving United States citizens that lost assets or freedom because of the internment practices.

## August 11, 1988

*Reparations are generally a good way for a wrong to be righted. Unfortunately, unless identified soon and righted early, they may put more salt in the wound than Band-Aids to cover it.*

*I remember the sentiment at the time and horror of the people on the West Coast because the attack in Hawaii was not very far away. I remember at the time being concerned that innocent people who have been living many years in the United States would be wrongly identified as the potential enemy. War is an ugly thing.*

On November 8, 1988, George H. W. Bush was elected President. President Reagan's Vice President rode the strong economy past the Democratic challenger Governor Michael Dukakis from Massachusetts.

Bush was able to garner a popular vote of over 53% and won the Electoral College vote with 426 votes to Dukakis' 111. Interestingly, while the Dukakis/Lloyd Bentsen ticket received 111 electoral votes, the Bentsen/Dukakis ticket received one vote.

The Democratic primaries were relatively wide open after an eight year Republican run in the white house by Ronald Reagan. Challengers knew that there was a strong likelihood that the public would be ready for a change in parties after two successive terms. Notable contenders were Joe Biden, Al Gore, Gary Hart and Jesse Jackson.

Notable Republican contenders were Bob Dole, Alexander Haig, Jack Kemp, Pat Robertson, and Don Rumsfeld.

At the Democratic Convention, as Arkansas Governor Bill Clinton was nominating Dukakis, his speech lasted so long that the most vociferous cheering happened after he uttered the words – "In closing…". Jesse Jackson was the only active candidate after the primaries and received 1,218.5 votes to Dukakis' 2,876.25.

## November 9, 1988

*Michael Dukakis has never really impressed me as a Governor, let alone a candidate for president. Do Democrats think that everyone who is from Massachusetts is a shoe-in for the presidency?*

*George Bush seems to be a very nice man. I am certain his wife keeps him in line; she seems like a very strong woman.*

*Reagan impressed me with his ability to get things done in office. He was fortunate to some degree that the economy could only go one direction when he took office, but he still needed to do the right things to make certain it turned around as quickly as possible and was in a position to be sustainable.*

# Chapter 31 – 1989

President Reagan signed the bill that provided the ability for the President to establish a new cabinet position and agency, the Department of Veterans Affairs. However, it was not until March 15, 1989 that President George H. W. Bush formally established the new department.

The department is charged with supporting veterans of armed services of the United States and their families. There are three components that the Department focuses on to provide support: healthcare, benefits, and burial support.

Some of the benefits that veterans are entitled to because of their service to the country are retirement compensation, education, loans, and death benefits.

The Department of Veteran Affairs manages over one hundred and thirty national cemeteries, as they are responsible for the management of all national cemeteries and various monument sites except Arlington National Cemetery.

# March 16, 1989

*It is an excellent message to veterans that there is an administrative body at the Federal level that has their backs. One of the most important roles of the President is to be the Commander in Chief of our armed services. This role is not meant to be simply another arrow in the quiver of the President to execute his or her personal agenda. It is important to take seriously, the sacrifice that members of the armed services make for their country.*

*I was fortunate to be a member of those armed services, which made me sensitive to the power and possible impact of that role. Sacrifices are not just time, but can be sacrifices of lives. My family was all too familiar with that as we lost my older brother Joe. The family, and especially my father, was devastated. Even though we understood the possible results of service, it truly hit home with Joe. Joe's death may have caused an increased focus on me, Bobby and Ted to focus on public service in the political rather than geopolitical battlefield.*

*The new Department of Veteran Affairs will be a way for this and future administrations to be able to provide the support to veterans unlike any that they have had in the past. This, at a minimum, can serve as a sign of gratitude from the people of the United States to veterans for their service. If managed well, the impact to service veterans will be that never again will the nation turn its collective backs on them as witnessed during and after the withdrawal from Vietnam.*

On December 3rd and 4th, 1989 President G. W. Bush and Soviet Premier Mikhail Gorbachev had a meeting that was called the Malta Summit. It was held two weeks after the fall of the Berlin Wall, a marker of the beginning of the unravelling of the Cold War.

The Malta Summit was an opportunity for leaders of the United States and Soviet Union to discuss how gracefully to continue the unravelling in a way that both countries' diplomats would look good in their corresponding countries while agreeing to continue to move toward peace.

The Cold War was an interesting "war" in that there were not battles as one would expect to see in a typical war, but rather more of a series of thumping of chests by both sides. Each of the thumps seeming to reverberate around the globe, with the sound of the thumping escalating with time.

The Malta Summit proceeded in without the typical chest thumping. However, no written agreements were reached at the Summit. The result was just a handshake, nice words for each other and promises to not start a hot war and cooperate better. Most accounts agree that this ended the children fighting in the sandbox.

## December 4, 1989

*A lot of emphasis was given to the Malta Summit between Gorbachev and Bush. However, it is obvious that the unwinding of the Soviet Union was happening well before the summit. In fact, I was a bit surprised that there were no documents signed. All politicians like the opportunity for a picture with a pen in their hand.*

One of the parts of the Anti-Drug Abuse Act of 1988 was the consent for the Executive Office of the President to establish a new bureaucratic office called the Office of National Drug Control Policy.

The goal of this office is to establish Federal policies to eliminate the creation, transportation and use of illegal drugs. The office is also charged with tracking and attempting to reduce drug-related crime and violence.

## December 21, 1989

*It is unfortunate that there is so much money involved in the underground drug market. People are getting rich from buying and selling drugs. The Office of National Drug Control Policy is an important step toward stopping illegal drugs from entering the country.*

*Ultimately, the issue of illegal drugs is a basic application of supply and demand. If the demand is high, then it becomes lucrative for more to be involved in the import, transportation and distribution of illegal drugs. The underground drug commerce is, in a sense, a typical example of American business. Unfortunately, it is an underground business in an area that tends to transform people that could be productive members of society to drags on society - if they have not killed themselves in the process.*

*Because it is driven by supply and demand, the only complete way to address the problem, since simply making it illegal does not work, is to attempt to reduce the demand. One option could be to legalize drugs and place a huge tax on them. Making them unaffordable to most people reduces demand because not as many people can buy them.*

*However, there would likely be unintended consequences. An underground market would flourish as drugs would continue to be illegally imported into the country and sold at an untaxed 'discount' to those who otherwise could not afford them. This would only tend to emphasize the divide between the rich and the poor. Distinguishing the taxed versus the untaxed drugs would be nearly impossible for enforcers, of the IRS.*

*Another way to reduce the demand for drugs is to encourage behaviors that do not rely on drug use. The premise that someone who strives to be a productive member of society to the extent that it is part of his or her character seems to be valid. It appears that those people who are less passionate about making a positive influence on society, tend to be more likely to have propensity toward drug use.*

*This is an area that government can be effective in addressing. If the leadership of the country focuses on providing opportunities for Americans to flourish in society and develop mindsets that give back to society through prosperity, then the great American experiment will continue to survive. However, if we allow divisiveness in terms of creating a fracturing of society by creating a bipolar situation where half the country gives and half the country takes, survival will be strained, if not ultimately impossible.*

*Government policies need to focus on reducing barriers for people to have the opportunity to give back to society and the personal character to want to give back - ask what you can do for your country.*

# Chapter 32 – 1990

## January 10, 1990

*I must be spending too much time paying attention to politics. As I reflect on much of what I am seeing and hearing, one of the realizations that I have come to is the fact that language is an important part of any political discussion.*

*As with all intellectual discourse, it is important to make certain there is a clear, unambiguous use of terminology. A few definitions have been bouncing around in my head that I wanted to write down to perhaps prevent future bouncing.*

*Spin - A quick and simple way to explain something that is in some way different from reality. The explanation may or may not have been test driven with a target audience to refine the message and words. This technique is sometimes used by the politicians themselves, but more often used by surrogates.*

*Surrogates - These are not politicians, but serve as mouthpieces for politicians. The value they bring is that they are not the politician. So, if they say something that is out of line or turns out to not fly well in the public airwaves, they can be easily replaced or discounted that they do not know what they are talking about.*

*Talking Points - These are a list of points that are periodically distributed to surrogates to be used to present common messages. Because of their wide distribution, it is important for surrogates when using them to vary the exact words so that the message does not sound like it is coming from a talking point. Three or more surrogates saying the same exact words begins to sound like marionettes – with and without strings. While the messages coming out of these political puppets may be consistent, when strung together by someone with an opposing viewpoint, they become somewhat comical. Fortunately for the surrogates, the general audience across the country does not hear enough of the surrogates repeating the talking points to be able to draw the puppet analogy. Talking points may or may not have been test driven by a target audience, depending on the speed they were produced and distributed.*

*Rhetoric - This is an interesting term, because it is the root of another interesting word – "rhetorical". A question is rhetorical if it is assumed that a response is not necessary. Given that, most everything coming out of the mouth of a politician or surrogate is rhetorical. A response is not necessary, or more importantly, not wanted. Therefore, the rhetoric that is often heard during political speeches is not meant to solicit a response. Perhaps commentators should not try.*

*Experts - Experts are individuals that do not have a name and are used to make a point. They may or may not actually exist and what is stated they say may or may not be swimming in a bucket of reality. They are used to lend credibility to a statement and effective because it is difficult to dispute their claims unless the experts are named, which rarely happens.*

President George H. W. Bush signed the Americans with Disabilities Act into law on July 26, 1990. This legislation protects persons with disabilities from discrimination. Under the language of the bill, disabilities are broadly defined as "a physical or mental impairment that substantially limits a major life activity."

An impairment that is simply corrected does not fall within the scope of this bill – such as corrective lenses for sight deficiencies or a hearing aid for hearing deficiencies.

Five areas fall into the scope of disability protection; employment, access to public entities, public accommodations, telecommunications, and a miscellaneous category.

Employment covers discrimination against a disabled person for gaining employment and calls for reasonable accommodations to be made that would allow the disabled to work.

Access to public entities covers transportation, access and reasonable accommodations to allow a disabled person the ability take advantage of the public service that is offered. An example is wheelchair access to a public library.

Public accommodations refer to the configuration or reconfiguration of a restaurant, hotel, arena, etc. so that someone with a disability may have access.

Telecommunications requires telecommunications companies to offer accommodations to hard of hearing or deaf people so they can use phone.

Miscellaneous provisions of the Act generally focus on the illegality of retaliation against a disabled person who identifies or complains against an accommodation failing to be provided.

### July 27, 1990

*The new American's with Disabilities Act is a breakthrough for the nation's disabled. Speaking from experience as a person who has been living with back issues most of his life; I know how important it is for there to be some basic accommodations for people with disabilities to live relatively normal lives.*

*I am surprised it has taken this long, given the fact that Franklin Roosevelt was confined to a wheelchair while serving the country's longest term as President. I suppose that had he been more open about his affliction, there would have been more of an outcry for the accommodations that this new Act calls for. Had there been term limits sooner and he known he was a lame duck (certainly no irony intended, but I gave myself a chuckle), he may have been more open knowing that his affliction would not prevent his reelection.*

*I look forward to seeing children and adults begin to feel better about their own disabilities. Particularly young men who found themselves disabled because of them having served their country. All disabled people should be treated equitably and fairly.*

# Chapter 33 – 1991

The Soviet Union was formally dissolved on December 26, 1991. Soviet President Mikhail Gorbachev resigned his position as leader of the combined nation on December 25, 1991. Twelve Soviet states remained, with the largest, Russia being led by Boris Yeltsin who won the Democratic elections with 57% of the vote.

During 1990, six republics dissolved formal ties from the mother ship – Soviet Union. They were Armenia, Georgia, and Moldova and the three Baltic states - Estonia, Latvia, and Lithuania.

### December 27, 1991

*Obviously, the United States had a significant hand in the break-up of the Soviet Union into smaller, less powerful states. While this signifies the end to the Cold War, it may only signify a pause in the Cold War. It is important to note that our desire to share the positive feelings we have about the freedoms that we have is not always shared by other cultures. Throughout history, large groups of people have been led by smaller groups of people that have managed one way or another, to gain power.*

*Freedom is hard. To achieve freedom, there cannot be a small group that has power over a larger one. If the representative democracy becomes less representative or less democratic, America could revert to a political system from which we came. It is the opportunity created for all to, within the boundaries of a common law, be liberated from control. If that fails, the default scenario will eventually prevail, which is dictatorial with polarized classes.*

*A simple example of this is the room in the house that has a television, a treadmill and a couch. Sam and Jerry are both unemployed. Sam, who is motivated to stay fit, spends more time on the treadmill than Jerry. Sam's passion for exercise is merged with the opportunity he has of having a treadmill. The result is that the treadmill gets used and Sam stays fit. The feedback that Sam received from his friends is that he looks good, which helps Sam stay motivated to continue to use the treadmill. Even though the couch and television are there as distractions, he only uses them after he uses the treadmill and maintains his fitness. Sam feels good about himself and during one of his treadmill sessions, decides on a skill that he wants to pursue, gets that skill, and ultimately gets a job using that skill.*

*Jerry, however, was told by his friends that exercise is not important. Since Jerry did not really like to sweat anyway, the opinions of his friends became easier to pay attention to and Jerry spent more time on the couch watching television. Occasionally, Jerry used the treadmill, but he still did not like to sweat and went back to the television and couch. Jerry was living with one of his friends that was also buying food for him, and telling him the treadmill was not necessary, so he was content.*

*At one point, Jerry decided that he was bored just lying on the couch and watching television. He was a bit jealous that Sam had been getting better jobs seemingly enjoying life more and getting involved in charitable events. Jerry decided to look for a job. By this time, Jerry's skills were no longer needed and he got frustrated and went back to the couch. It was easier than working to achieve his goal.*

*Just like laziness in fitness, expansion of the mind, and building of character can result in the default scenario of television and a couch, so can the broader laziness of a nation result in the default of allowing someone else to control everything, trading liberty and freedom for the ability to not have to work for it or think about it. I hope we never achieve the default.*

# Chapter 34 – 1992

In April of 1992, the acquittal of four Los Angeles Police Department officers spurred broad rioting throughout Los Angeles. The riots, also called the Rodney King Riots, were named for the recipient of an event that was described to consist of excessive force and assault to subdue Rodney King after a high-speed police pursuit. The action of subduing King was videotaped and quickly hit the national news cycles.

The six days of rioting started on April 29, 1992 after the announcement of the acquittal verdict of the police officers. Members of the California Army National Guard and United States Marines from Camp Pendleton were called in as the riots were too much for the Los Angeles police department to handle. At the end of the six days, there were over fifty killed, over two thousand injured and over a billion dollars of property damage.

### May 9, 1992

*The Los Angeles Riots were another challenging event close to my home. Tensions in the south side of Los Angeles are almost like a powder keg constantly sitting ready for any kind of spark to ignite it.*

*It is unfortunate that the situation was so far out of control. The constant display of the video with the police attempting to detain Mr. King may have contributed to the situation. Police will need to, in the future, consider that anything they do may be recorded when they are in the process of protecting the citizens.*

*Often, the split second decisions that police officers need to make are not accurately recorded on a tape. The physical actions may be recorded, but what is going on in the minds of people involved cannot be accurately recorded.*

The opportunity for Congress to give themselves raises as their terms are ending was eliminated with the Twenty-seventh Amendment to the Constitution.

From time to time, Congress votes pay raises to themselves. This makes sense, because if they were making the same salary they were paid in 1789, they would make $6 per day. Of course, on the other hand, a $6 daily salary may prevent a Congressman from making a profession out of his post instead of a passion.

Complaints about congressional salaries and salary increases are almost as old as the Constitution. In fact, the first attempt to control their ability to set their own salaries was supposed to be part of the original bill of rights, but never fully ratified.

On May 7, 1992, Michigan was the thirty-ninth and deciding State to ratify the Twenty-seventh Amendment to the Constitution. The text of the Amendment stated that adjustments to Congressional salaries can only take effect at the beginning of a Congressional term.

## May 8, 1992

*The ability of Congress to vote themselves raises reminds me of the writings of John Adams as he describes Congressmen, "It is not true, in fact, that any people ever existed who love the public better than themselves."*

With help from Ross Perot taking almost 19% of the popular vote, Arkansas Governor Bill Clinton won over President Bush in the 1992 Presidential elections.

Clinton garnered only 43% of the popular vote, but with the dilution of the vote by Ross Perot, managed to win the Electoral College by a 370 to 168 margin.

President Bush did not have a lot of competition during the primaries. By the Republican convention, only two other candidates got any votes, which amounted to less than one percent of the total.

Notable challengers for Clinton by the time the dust settled after the primaries were Jerry Brown from California and Paul Tsongas from Massachusetts.

## November 4, 1992

*The power of a third party candidate to take enough votes from one party or another to affect the results of an election as dramatically as Mr. Perot was able to do is amazing. Perhaps the nation has become complex enough to warrant the need for more than two parties. I am not certain that the current structure of political funding and State voting laws encourages more than two parties today, but it is interesting to consider how a strong third party may play out. Rather than focusing on more than fifty percent of the Electoral College to win, the focus could be on achieving more electoral votes than the other two candidate (assuming three major parties). Another option could be a narrowing of the field vote followed by a run-off election.*

228

*The results of this election would not have been different, but if people truly believe that their votes for a third party candidate are not 'wasted', they may be more inclined to choose someone different.*

*It would be interesting to see what would happen if there was a candidate that was precisely in the middle of the political spectrum. The pendulum that seems to cyclically swing from left to right may be challenged by a force that stops it in the center. Liberals and Conservatives are often seen by many people as radically different from their point of view and they are forced to choose the one that happens to agree with more of the views that they think are important.*

*If a candidate were able to unlock the fortresses of Republicans and Democrats and have a majority of opinions that align with the highest priorities of the majority of American, that candidate may have a chance to win. Mr. Perot seemed to position himself in just that light, garnering a large percentage of the 'middle of the road' voters, mostly from the conservative side. Had he been a little more balanced in his approach, he may have made the challenge between President Bush and Governor Clinton even tighter. Who knows, the results that Mr. Perot was able to attain may encourage another third party candidate in the future.*

*Clinton seems to be a hard worker; he seems to have what it takes to be an effective President.*

# Chapter 35 – 1993

President Clinton signed the North American Free Trade Agreement into law on December 8, 1993. This agreement was between the United States, Canada and Mexico and called for the reduction of barriers for easy trade amongst the three countries.

Essentially, the North American Free Trade Agreement reduced tariffs and enhanced the ability for workers to move amongst the three countries easier to work.

### December 9, 1993

*Many times, I had leaders of various industries in my office discussing the challenges of their particular situation – to the extent that it began to feel like a revolving door. There was at least one common theme to the challenges they described – competition.*

*At first, I thought they were describing competition with other American companies. Nevertheless, almost to a person, they were describing a situation where tariffs and regulations made competition with foreign companies very difficult.*

*I understand the importance of the existence of fair trade between countries. Fair trade helps each country sell goods and services that they have in excess and buy goods and services in areas of deficit. One country does not need to manufacture everything if there is freedom and equity in trade.*

*The Swiss are fine artisans of watches and pocketknives. They have a long history in developing the skills needed to exceed the quality that other countries can produce. We produce more food than we need and can export to other countries giving them less expensive choices with greater amounts. We send food to Australia, the Australians send raw materials to the Swiss, and the Swiss send watches to the United States. Everything works.*

*However, when a country established high tariffs on imports of foreign goods because they are trying to encourage domestic production, the prices become less competitive and exports to and imports from foreign countries diminish.*

# Chapter 36 – 1994

On May 19, 1994, Jackie Kennedy Onassis died from a non-Hodgkins form of cancer. She was sixty-four years old.

### May 20, 1994

*I cannot say that I did not weep when I heard the news that Jackie had died. For the last thirty years, my heart has been heavy that I have not seen my family. If I had it all over to do again, I would have taken the bullets in Dallas.*

*Many times I have dreamed about having Frank and his team bring them to see me, but I know that would not only be dangerous, but would not be fair to them. They have their lives, and they need to live them.*

*I hope that Jackie always believed that not only did I love her, but also that she was the glue that kept me together. Her cool head and quiet demeanor may have seemed to others as a divergent conflict with the appearance of my behavior sometimes. However, everyone should know that my heart always stayed true to Jackie.*

*I recall one night that I was struggling over the Cuba issues. Jackie was reading a book and I was pacing the floor - likely wringing my hands and mumbling. Quietly, without me noticing, she got up. By the time I was paying attention, she had opened a window. She motioned for me to join her by the window.*

*She told me to close my eyes and take a deep breath. I did. A large breath, filling my lungs and then a slow exhale as the night air escaped my lips. Then she said, "Mr. President, you may be the leader of the most powerful nation on Earth, but you are also a husband and a father which means you are human. You are surrounded by excellent support and the only real mistake you could possibly make is not by the decision you make, but the decision you do not make."*

*With that, we stood there without making a sound. She then turned and went to bed. I stood there for a few minutes longer, thinking about her words and how she delivered them. Then, I shut the window and joined her in bed. It was the best night's sleep I had in weeks.*

*The next day I woke up refreshed and with a clear head. It may have been my imagination, but everyone around me seemed to notice that I was different. My head was clear, I listened to what everyone had to say, and I made decisions.*

*I love you Jackie.*

The general election of 1994 saw Republicans gain fifty-four seats in the House and eight seats in the Senate. Even House Speaker Foley lost his seat during the Republican swing, which was the first time a sitting Speaker lost a reelection since the Lincoln days.

With the swing, Newt Gingrich was able to elevate himself from Minority Whip to Speaker of the House. In his Contract With America, Gingrich promised to bring a dozen important pieces of legislation to the floor of the House in the first one hundred days of Republican control.

# November 9, 1994

The election results of 1994 were another example of the pendulum of politics, with the Republicans gaining control of the House. The House of Representatives is the better representation of the thinking of the people as they are up for reelection every two years so they need to generally be more in tune with their constituencies that the Senators.

I was not very surprised with the outcome of this election. The general election in 1992 was skewed because Ross Perot garnered so much support. It is still definitely a two party system. Moreover, unless there is significant public outcry, I do not see that changing any time soon.

To add a third party could make elections very interesting. Imagine if there were three candidates, all equally popular. It could take a number of votes by the Electoral College before a victor is decided. In addition, if the Electoral College cannot decide, be prepared for a bit of a constitutional crisis.

The reason why I do not see anything more than two major parties is the nature of choice. Most all issues have two sides, a yay and a nay. Until there are many issues that somehow come up with a third decision criteria, we may be stuck with what we have.

# Chapter 37 – 1995

Rose Kennedy was married to Jack's father Joe on July 25, 1915. She was certainly the matriarch of the Kennedy family and lived a long and fruitful life. Her roots in New England were deep. Her father was once the mayor of Boston. She and Joe had nine children – Joe, Jack, Rosemary, Kick, Eunice, Pat, Bobby, Jean and Ted.

Rose did her best to keep the family together, but the culture of being a Kennedy always seemed to be one of living life on the edge. Still, Rose was always proud of her children. Perhaps they just did not have all the luck of the Irish, but they seemed to live and die hard.

On January 22, 1995, Rose died of pneumonia. She had been confined to a wheelchair for over a decade after a stroke.

### January 23, 1995

*I just got word that my mother died yesterday. May she rest in peace.*

*One of my fond memories of my Mother and I was one day when I was very young my Mother and I were at a park. There were some people gathering down a hill and I encouraged my Mother to take me there. As we were approaching the group, more and more people were gathering, forming a circle and there was someone moving around in the middle. There was also music.*

*When we joined the circle, I noticed that the someone moving inside the circle was a monkey. He was wearing a red and black outfit with a little matching hat. He reminded me of the bellman that always said hello to me when we were downtown New York City.*

*He was on what looked like a leash and attached to an older man who was turning a crank, which made music. My Mother explained that the man was an organ grinder. I watched intently as the monkey was going from person to person. When I asked what he was doing, I was told that he was collecting money for the organ grinder since was making such nice music.*

*I hadn't paid much attention to the monetary transaction as a reason for the organ grinder to turn the crank, until I figured out that in order to get the monkey to pay attention to me, I needed to participate in that transaction.*

*I then saw that people would hold a penny in their hand, the organ grinder would quickly flip his hand toward the person holding the penny and the monkey would go and get it. When the monkey retrieved the coin, he tipped his little hat and took the coin back to the organ grinder.*

*I wanted in on that!*

*I asked my Mother if she had any pennies. She rooted around in the bottom of her purse and recovered a handful of pennies. We managed to get to the inner circle and I took one of the pennies and held it up with a smile of pride and expectation. As pre-orchestrated, the organ grinder flipped his hand toward me, and the monkey came over and took the coin right out of my hand - it tickled a little.*

*This was great. I took another penny out of my Mother's hand and held it out for the monkey. Same procedure and I was relieved of my penny by the hat-tipping monkey. I followed this process a few more times. The rest of the people in the circle were just watching and laughing at the interaction between the monkey and me. I think they may have been enamored with seeing the little kid not much bigger than the monkey.*

*On the fifth time, the monkey must have learned where the source of the pennies was because he walked past me, grabbed the rest of the pennies from my mother's hand, tipped his hat and took them back to the organ grinder. This time, the organ grinder tipped HIS hat. Everyone laughed. At first, I was upset that my supply of pennies had been extinguished, but I laughed with everyone else.*

*Years later, upon reflection, the organ grinder could have had "US Government" written on his hat and the monkey "IRS".*

*Goodbye Mom.*

# Chapter 38 – 1996

## November 27, 1996

*I was thinking about the need for a more fair treatment by government of couples that are not necessarily a man and a woman. The challenge is that both sides of the debate have a fair point regarding this issue, but the points are not able to cohabitate.*

*One side of the debate is adamant that a marriage is between a man and a woman. These debaters state, and it could be argued both ways, that the Bible calls for marriage between a man and a woman with no mention of any other options.*

*The Biblical book of Genesis states that God created a man and a woman and told them to multiply. While this may be important for successful procreation and expansion of the species, it does not necessarily specify marriage.*

*Also in Genesis, the scripture describes the rib taken from man to create woman so he has someone to go to when he leaves his father and mother and to "become one flesh". This appears to be a direct statement of becoming one flesh between a man and a woman, but does not necessarily exclude any other options.*

*There are other references to the relationship between a man and a woman. However, there is no mention that is the exclusive example of the point being made, which is really one of fidelity. Malachi describes the woman as a companion and wife by covenant. Hebrews warns that the marriage bed should not be defiled by adulterous behavior.*

*Interestingly, there is one very well-known passage described in multiple biblical chapters that where, while marriage was contemplated, it was not necessary in the resulting outcome – the birth of Jesus.*

*These are just a few of many examples of mention of marriage in the Bible, which is why students of the Bible are so adamant about who the participants should be in a marriage, because that is the interpretation they have been taught.*

*The ultimate question is, "How should government respond to this issue?" The answer should be easy, but has eluded politicians and the public for years.*

*Marriage is a religious term that should be reserved for religious use.*

*The Constitution provides the answer in its insistence that there be a separation between Church and State. Government should leave the Church alone and the Church should leave government alone.*

*So, for the purposes of government benefits, like taxes, a partnership with assets, and social benefits, the government should not engage in religious ceremonies. They should be reserved for religious entities. Rather, government should be concerned with the establishment of civil unions between two people regardless of who they are as long as they follow the lawful contract and process of merger and separation. Government can continue to vest the power of the civil merger with anyone that successfully passes the appropriate licensure. Government should not be responsible for, nor issue marriage certificates, as they are religious artifacts. Moreover, the only way to receive the government benefits or recognition should only be to officially enter into the civil union, for everyone.*

*Religious marriage can then remain the sole responsibility of religious organizations, which should be able to determine qualifications of marriage under their particular beliefs.*

*I am not certain why it took an old man to figure this out.*

# Chapter 39 – The Final Journey

## July 4, 1999

*I have not felt like writing in the past several years. Partially because there was not a lot of interesting thing to write about and partly because my health has not been as strong as it once was. As my health continues to deteriorate, I wanted, as one last request, to talk to my children.*

*I have talked the Secret Service to in to setting up a meeting with John Junior. As I am told, based on security challenges, the best place for me to meet him is at Martha's Vineyard. He will be there for a wedding of his cousin Rory. The Secret Service wants to maintain the secrecy of my California bunker in case there is a need for it in the future.*

*Times continue to be a struggle for the country and you cannot well predict behaviors nor thoroughly protect the President. The date was set for my trip to the East Coast. I have not been to that side of the country since November 22, 1964. I was not only looking forward to the trip, but to talking to my son, perhaps for the last time.*

## July 14, 1999

*I remember the last time John and I had an alone moment. We were sitting on the floor of the living room at the White House. There was a tin house that my father gave me when I was young. It was as big as a basketball and looked like some of the houses on Martha's Vineyard. It was given to my father by one of his friends. It was hand crafted and painted. John seemed to like it as much as I did.*

*The chimney of the house was made into a slot, were you could put money. It was one of the most interesting banks I ever saw. After my father gave it to me, he used to give me silver dollars when I did my chores or got good grades in school. Every time I got one of those silver dollars, I put it in the house bank.*

*The house was about three-fourths full of silver dollars – Mercury and Liberty coins. John used to like it when I shook it because it made a lot of noise, the clinging of all of those dollars against the sides of the tin house. He asked me to open it, but I always showed him the bottom of the house where the tinsmith who made it had soldered the opening closed.*

*As we sat on the floor and he was talking about his day, I saw him keep looking up at that bank. Finally, I said, "So John, what do you think about trying to get that bank open?" His eyes lit up and he ran over to get the bank. It was so heavy he could not lift it. I got up and picked it up. When I did, he saw the plug in the bottom soldered shut. He asked, "How are we going to open it up?" I told him that I did not know, but I would try.*

*I had a pocketknife in a drawer in the other room, so I retrieved is and came back to tackle the bank. Fortunately, it was only soldered in four places around the plug. I was able to chip away at the solder and free two of the four connections. Once they were loosened, I was able to work one other connection loose and bend the plug open.*

*I held the bank about waist high and started to shake the coins out. John started clapping and soon Jackie was at the door wondering what all the noise was. Coins kept pouring out into a large pile on the floor. Once I got every coin out, which John insisted on doing, I put the bank back on the shelf and sat down on the floor with John and the pile of silver dollars between us.*

*Then, John sat quietly as I started to stack them. For what seemed like a half hour but likely shorter, I stacked and stacked silver dollars into about ten stacks, all about the same size. About half way through, I handed one to John and told him to hold onto it so he could put the last coin on the stack. John just sat there are watched as I stacked the coins.*

*I finally was finished and reminded him that he needed to put the last one on the pile. John leaned forward, lost his balance as he was placing the silver dollar on the tallest stack, and fell right into the piles, scattering all the dollars all over the floor.*

*Tears welled up in his eyes and he looked up at me to see my reaction to his demolition of all the work I had just done. I started laughing. Shortly, he started laughing too. I said, "Well John, how about some ice cream before we pick up all these dollars." By the time we got back, Jackie had picked up all the coins and put them back in the house. She said it was time for John to go to bed.*

## July 15, 1999

*The trip across country was very enjoyable. I had almost forgotten the beauty that extends, as the song goes, from sea to shining sea. Technology has changed many things, but the beauty and friendliness of the American people has surely not diminished.*

  *I was told that the plan was that the Secret Service was to contact John the day before he was to come to Martha's Vineyard. They were going to explain to him that I was still alive, was in poor health, but wanted to see him before I died. I also want to see Caroline, but her schedule will prevent me from seeing her for a few days, and then - back to the California bunker.*

With a very shaky hand, Kennedy wrote his last journal entry

## July 17, 1999

  *I was awakened by Frank early this morning. He explained that everything was going as expected until late last night. Rather than driving to Martha's Vineyard as was suggested, John had decided to fly his plane, as he was anxious to talk to me. Apparently, this proved to be a serious error in judgment. The weather was hazy, John was not licensed to fly on instruments and the plane went down. John, his wife and one other person died.*

The grief was all JFK could handle. Two days after receiving word that his son had died on July 16, 1999, President Kennedy shut his eyes for the final time at the age of eighty-two - one day before he was to meet Caroline.

  Fortunately, the Secret Service had not yet contacted Caroline. This was likely a wise decision as the knowledge that her father was actually alive all these years and she never knew, may have been devastating to her. The odd luck of the Kennedy family - the extreme highs and lows - continues.

  As with most everything else with the Secret Service, plans and preparations were already made for this inevitable day. About a decade or so prior to this date, a tunnel was dug at Arlington

National Cemetery. Jack made his final journey through the tunnel after a brief, but very ceremonial, send off by several members of the Secret Service regimen that would move his body through the tunnel. Some of the same words were used that were uttered at the public ceremony. Therefore, finally, now three feet above President Kennedy's body double is entombed the real body of the 35th President of the United States, John Fitzgerald Kennedy.

"One person can make a difference, and everyone should try."

John Fitzgerald Kennedy

# Epilogue: Inaugural Speech

The following is the text from President Kennedy's speech delivered on Friday, January 20, 1961. Chief Justice Earl Warren officiated the oath of office. Robert Frost read one of his poems – "The Gift Outright".

*Vice President Johnson, Mr. Speaker, Mr. Chief Justice, President Eisenhower, Vice President Nixon, President Truman, reverend clergy, fellow citizens:*

*We observe today not a victory of party, but a celebration of freedom -- symbolizing an end, as well as a beginning -- signifying renewal, as well as change. For I have sworn before you and Almighty God the same solemn oath our forebears prescribed nearly a century and three-quarters ago.*

*The world is very different now. For man holds in his mortal hands the power to abolish all forms of human poverty and all forms of human life. Yet the same revolutionary beliefs for which our forebears fought are still at issue around the globe -- the belief that the rights of man come not from the generosity of the state, but from the hand of God.*

*We dare not forget today that we are the heirs of that first revolution. Let the word go forth from this time and place, to friend and foe alike, that the torch has been passed to a new generation of Americans -- born in this century, tempered by war, disciplined by a hard and bitter peace, proud of our ancient heritage, and unwilling to witness or permit the slow undoing of those human rights to which this nation has always been committed, and to which we are committed today at home and around the world.*

*Let every nation know, whether it wishes us well or ill, that we shall pay any price, bear any burden, meet any hardship, support any friend, oppose any foe, to assure the survival and the success of liberty.*

*This much we pledge -- and more.*

*To those old allies whose cultural and spiritual origins we share, we pledge the loyalty of faithful friends. United there is little we cannot do in a host of cooperative ventures. Divided there is little we can do -- for we dare not meet a powerful challenge at odds and split asunder.*

*To those new states whom we welcome to the ranks of the free, we pledge our word that one form of colonial control shall not have passed away merely to be replaced by a far more iron tyranny. We shall not always expect to find them supporting our view. But we shall always hope to find them strongly supporting their own freedom -- and to remember that, in the past, those who foolishly sought power by riding the back of the tiger ended up inside.*

*To those people in the huts and villages of half the globe struggling to break the bonds of mass misery, we pledge our best efforts to help them help themselves, for whatever period is required -- not because the Communists may be doing it, not because we seek their votes, but because it is right. If a free society cannot help the many who are poor, it cannot save the few who are rich.*

*To our sister republics south of our border, we offer a special pledge: to convert our good words into good deeds, in a new alliance for progress, to assist free men and free governments in casting off the chains of poverty. But this peaceful revolution of hope cannot become the prey of hostile powers. Let all our neighbors know that we shall join with them to oppose aggression or subversion anywhere in the Americas. And let every other power know that this hemisphere intends to remain the master of its own house.*

*To that world assembly of sovereign states, the United Nations, our last best hope in an age where the instruments of war have far outpaced the instruments of peace, we renew our pledge of support -- to prevent it from becoming merely a forum for invective, to strengthen its shield of the new and the weak, and to enlarge the area in which its writ may run.*

*Finally, to those nations who would make themselves our adversary, we offer not a pledge but a request: that both sides begin anew the quest for peace, before the dark powers of destruction unleashed by science engulf all humanity in planned or accidental self-destruction.*

*We dare not tempt them with weakness. For only when our arms are sufficient beyond doubt can we be certain beyond doubt that they will never be employed.*

*But neither can two great and powerful groups of nations take comfort from our present course -- both sides overburdened by the cost of modern weapons, both rightly alarmed by the steady spread of the deadly atom, yet both racing to alter that uncertain balance of terror that stays the hand of mankind's final war.*

*So let us begin anew -- remembering on both sides that civility is not a sign of weakness, and sincerity is always subject to proof. Let us never negotiate out of fear, but let us never fear to negotiate.*

*Let both sides explore what problems unite us instead of belaboring those problems which divide us.*

*Let both sides, for the first time, formulate serious and precise proposals for the inspection and control of arms, and bring the absolute power to destroy other nations under the absolute control of all nations.*

*Let both sides seek to invoke the wonders of science instead of its terrors. Together let us explore the stars, conquer the deserts, eradicate disease, tap the ocean depths, and encourage the arts and commerce.*

*Let both sides unite to heed, in all corners of the earth, the command of Isaiah -- to "undo the heavy burdens, and [to] let the oppressed go free."*

*And, if a beachhead of cooperation may push back the jungle of suspicion, let both sides join in creating a new endeavor -- not a new balance of power, but a new world of law -- where the strong are just, and the weak secure, and the peace preserved.*

*All this will not be finished in the first one hundred days. Nor will it be finished in the first one thousand days; nor in the life of this Administration; nor even perhaps in our lifetime on this planet. But let us begin.*

*In your hands, my fellow citizens, more than mine, will rest the final success or failure of our course. Since this country was founded, each generation of Americans has been summoned to give testimony to its national loyalty. The graves of young Americans who answered the call to service surround the globe.*

*Now the trumpet summons us again -- not as a call to bear arms, though arms we need -- not as a call to battle, though embattled we are -- but a call to bear the burden of a long twilight struggle, year in and year out, "rejoicing in hope; patient in tribulation,"[2] a struggle against the common enemies of man: tyranny, poverty, disease, and war itself.*

*Can we forge against these enemies a grand and global alliance, North and South, East and West, that can assure a more fruitful life for all mankind? Will you join in that historic effort?*

*In the long history of the world, only a few generations have been granted the role of defending freedom in its hour of maximum danger. I do not shrink from this responsibility -- I welcome it. I do not believe that any of us would exchange places with any other people or any other generation. The energy, the faith, the devotion which we bring to this endeavor will light our country and all who serve it. And the glow from that fire can truly light the world.*

*And so, my fellow Americans, ask not what your country can do for you; ask what you can do for your country.*

*My fellow citizens of the world, ask not what America will do for you, but what together we can do for the freedom of man.*

*Finally, whether you are citizens of America or citizens of the world, ask of us here the same high standards of strength and sacrifice which we ask of you. With a good conscience our only sure reward, with history the final judge of our deeds, let us go forth to lead the land we love, asking His blessing and His help, but knowing that here on earth God's work must truly be our own.*

# Postface

It would not be surprising if the extremes of the political spectrum, whether ultra-liberal or ultra-conservative, will not appreciate this book. The intent was not to highlight one side or another. It may be interesting to document any reactions, attacks, or criticisms as a source for a subsequent prose.

The target audience is more in between the extreme swings of the pendulum. It was written to be targeted to 'We the People' of the middle who get whacked in the head as the pendulum swings violently from one side to the other. One of these days, we may be successful in grabbing the pendulum like a brass ring on a merry-go-round and holding it still in the middle for a while.

www.ingramcontent.com/pod-product-compliance
Lightning Source LLC
Chambersburg PA
CBHW070840310526
45793CB00010B/45